Twayne's United States Authors Series

EDITOR OF THIS VOLUME

Warren French

Indiana University

Edward Lewis Wallant

TUSAS 319

EDWARD LEWIS WALLANT

By DAVID GALLOWAY

University of the Ruhr,
Bochum, Germany

TWAYNE PUBLISHERS
A DIVISION OF G. K. HALL & CO., BOSTON

Galloway, David D
Edward Lewis Wallant.

(Twayne's United States authors series; TUSAS 319)
Bibliography: p. 163–66
Includes index.
1.   Wallant, Edward Lewis, 1926–1962—Criticism and
interpretation.
PS3573.A434Z68   813'.5'4   [B]   79–4057
ISBN O–8057–7250–2

For Dan Wickenden

Contents

About the Author

David Galloway is Ordinarius Professor of American Studies at the Ruhr University in Bochum, Germany. He has taught at the Universities of Hamburg, Sussex, Case Western Reserve, Cairo, Riyad and Trinity College Dublin, and is a frequent guest lecturer in Africa and the Middle East. His critical works include *The Absurd Hero, Henry James: The Portrait of a Lady,* and the Penguin edition of Edgar Allan Poe; he is also the author of three novels—*Melody Jones, A Family Album,* and *Lamaar Ransom: Private Eye.* As guest curator and advisor, Dr. Galloway has worked for many years with art galleries and museums, and until recently was on leave from the Ruhr University to act as Chief Curator of the new Tehran Museum of Contemporary Art.

Preface

While more than a decade now intervenes, I still recall the
excitement of reading the novels of Edward Lewis Wallant when
they first appeared. Here, I felt, was an American original;
inventive, robust, informed by a profound compassion, his novels
significantly enriched my own vision of the world. Furthermore,
the author's increasing command of fictional craft seemed to
promise even more accomplished works to come. Thus, Wallant's
early death seemed to me then, as now, a tragic loss for American
letters. When, shortly after the author's death, I was preparing a
book entitled *The Absurd Hero* for publication, I remarked in the
preface that

in electing to discuss the work of Updike, Styron, Bellow, and Salinger
in light of [Camus's] theories, I have excluded, of course, other writers
who might have been considered with equal fruitfulness. John Hawkes
and Edward Lewis Wallant seem to me the most significant contemporary omissions, and I particularly regret that Wallant receives only
brief reference in *The Absurd Hero;* but his four brilliant and moving
novels surely qualify him for a book in his own right.

Having now more intensively explored Wallant's published and
unpublished works, I feel yet more strongly that a close analysis
of his writings has much to tell us about the craft of writing, the
nature of his heroism, and the spiritual condition of man at mid-
century.

This study of Wallant's fiction begins with his early, largely
unpublished short stories, and continues through the unfinished
novel, *Tannenbaum's Journey,* on which he was working at the
time of his death. Such a chronological approach to the work
best reveals the extraordinary development of Wallant's narrative skills, and his movement from a troubled, tragic vision of
experience to a robustly comic optimism. Unpublished short
stories and novels have been examined here in some detail, for
the considerable light they throw on Wallant's literary appren-

ticeship, and variant drafts of the published novels are discussed where they serve to clarify the author's intentions. Wallant did not live to produce a work that was, from the aesthetic standpoint, entirely adequate to his vision. He was still, at the time of his death, learning the basic skills of his craft, though with remarkable sureness and speed and a contagious humor that sparkles through the pages of his later works. He must, ultimately, be judged a minor writer, but one who nonetheless made his own powerfully original contribution to American letters. The essential outlines of this achievement are sketched in Chapter 9.

The following analysis of the novels stresses the author's concerns with such familiar contemporary themes as the erosion of the family, the encroachments of technology, the loss of substaining contact with nature, and the growing isolation of the individual. But it would be misleading to underscore such themes too boldly, for there is a timeless quality to Wallant's depiction of the search for an authentic self—one which he enriches through allusion to Jewish, Christian, and pagan mythologies. Similarly, while it is often necessary to explicate particular allusions to Jewish ritual in order to appreciate individual episodes in the novels, the spiritual impulse which informs Wallant's vision ultimately transcends religion and creed. There is, perhaps, no surer indication of a writer's stature than this ability to fuse the particular and the general—to be distinctly "of his time" and for all time. Wallant's recurrent subject was man's capacity for spiritual regeneration, and he sounded it with increasing joy and authority throughout his brief literary career.

To appreciate that joyful affirmation, the reader must consider the Chassidic values and religious rituals which give it form. I have also found it instructive to compare Wallant's achievement with that of such Jewish contemporaries as Saul Bellow and Bernard Malamud. In the postwar years, black and Jewish writers have played a central role in establishing the distinctive resonance of the contemporary novel. It is hardly surprising that, at a time when man often feels estranged from community and tradition, the black and the Jew should speak with such authority and conviction of that modern condition. As Ralph Ellison's nameless hero remarks, "Who knows but that, on the lower frequencies, I speak for you?" Any of Wallant's dangling men might pose the same question, and it is the degree to which they dramatize the spiritual dilemma of contemporary man which insures their relevance to any study of the modern literary temperament. Indeed, Wallant's name frequently occurs in general studies of postwar American writing, but beyond a handful of critical articles and three unpublished doctoral dissertations, there has been no extensive analysis of his novels. This book, through detailed explications of the works in order of their composition, attempts both to illuminate Wallant's unique accomplishments and to establish his place within the diverse currents of the American literary imagination.

My own insights into Wallant's fiction were greatly enhanced by conversations with his widow, Mrs. Joyce Malkin, and with Dan Wickenden, his editor at Harcourt, Brace. Thanks to Mrs. Malkin's interest in this project, I was permitted to examine the Wallant manuscripts even before they were made publicly available to scholars and critics; Donald Gallup and the staff at the Beinecke Library at Yale University assisted me in these researches. Of the many friends and colleagues who shared with me their memories of Edward Lewis Wallant—often at painful price as they confronted once more the awful, wasteful suddenness of his death—John A. Williams and Ann McGovern were particularly generous. In puzzling out the sequence of Wallant's unpublished manuscripts, establishing the sequence of variant drafts of the published novels, and determining the occasional real-life counterpart for some of the fictional characters, I repeatedly turned to Wallant's gifted editor, Dan Wickenden. This book is dedicated to him not merely as a token of my own gratitude, but in acknowledgment of the key role he played in encouraging, developing, and refining Wallant's literary skills. He has been for me, as he was for Edward Lewis Wallant, a valued friend and respected critic.

Acknowledgments

All quotations from Wallant's published works are cited with the permission of Harcourt, Brace and Company, New York. References to the unpublished manuscripts are by permission of the Estate of Edward Lewis Wallant and its executrix, Mrs. Joyce Malkin.

Chronology

1926   October 19. Edward Lewis Wallant born, New Haven, Connecticut.

1944   Graduated, New Haven High School; briefly enrolled at the University of Connecticut; joins the U.S. Navy and serves until the end of World War II as Gunner's Mate, European Theater of Operations.

1947   Discharged from the Navy; marries Joyce Fromkin, whom he has known since childhood; enrolls in Pratt Instutute.

1948   Moves to Brooklyn, New York.

1950   Graduated from Pratt Institute; employed by L. W. Frohlich advertising agency, New York; begins to take courses in creative writing with Harold Glicksberg and Don M. Wolfe at the New School for Social Research; moves to New Rochelle, New York.

1952   Son Scott born.

1953   Employed by Doyle, Kitchen and McCormick advertising agency, New York; moves to Norwalk, Connecticut.

1954   Daughter Leslie born.

1955   First short story, "I Held Back My Hand," published.

1957   Employed as an art director by McCann Erikson advertising agency, New York—the position he held at the time of his death in 1962; daughter Kim born.

1960   *The Human Season;* receives the Jewish Book Council Fiction Award; attends Breadloaf Writers Conference.

1961   *The Pawnbroker.*

1962   Travels for three months in Europe (chiefly in Italy and Spain) on Guggenheim Fellowship; December 5, dies of a stroke resulting from an aneurism of the brain.

1963   *The Tenants of Moonbloom* published posthumously.

1965   *The Children at the Gate* published posthumously.

CHAPTER 1

A Commonplace History

WHEN Edward Lewis Wallant died in 1962, at the age of thirty-six, he had published only two novels. Nonetheless, several critics lamented the loss of such a "promising" writer— even those who knew nothing of the two brilliant novels that would be published posthumously in 1963 and 1964. If this quartet of tragicomic works seems a modest oeuvre, one must remember that the books were written in little more than two years, and in circumstances that would scarcely seem encouraging for the fledgling novelist.

Indeed, nothing in the commonplace history of Wallant's life adequately accounts for the literary brilliance of his late writings. Born in New Haven, Connecticut, on October 19, 1926, Edward Lewis Wallant grew up in a shabby if respectable middle-class neighborhood. His father, a veteran of World War I crippled by mustard gas, died of tuberculosis when Eddie was only six. The father was almost continuously hospitalized in his final years, so that the invalid and tubercular fathers who appear and reappear in Wallant's writings are embodiments of imagination rather than memory. An only child, the boy was raised by his mother and two aunts, all of whom doted on this heir but lacked the means to indulge him. For a time, the boy also had contact with a Russian-born grandfather: "I was the grandchild who listened when he talked about the old country," Wallant later remarked. Those childhood recollections would emerge with special vividness in *The Human Season*, Wallant's first published novel.

Wallant attended New Haven High School, graduating in 1944. As an adolescent he held a variety of odd jobs—as plumber's assistant, delivery boy for a pharmacy across from the Catholic hospital in New Haven, and hot-dog salesman at Eli football games. Following his graduation, and though he had never shown particular academic brilliance, he enrolled briefly at the

University of Connecticut but soon resigned to join the navy. In the first eighteen years of Wallant's life the sole hint at his later sense of literary vocation was his interest in reading. As an adolescent he devoured works like Edgar Wallace's *Flying Squad,* Howard Pease's *The Jinx Ship,* and Edgar Rice Burroughs's *Tarzan of the Apes.* By chance, *The Adventures of Huckleberry Finn* made its way onto this list and, as the author later remarked, "lingered with me with the queer power of someone I had actually known." As the currency of good prose began to drive out the bad, Wallant felt himself entering a new world: "I played games of eating, games in which I was grateful for the food I otherwise took for granted, all because of Robinson Crusoe's ordeal. I was beginning to appreciate and to *require* art." Among the books that had profound impact on his own sensibility were *The Brothers Karamazov, Jude the Obscure, Look Homeward, Angel,* and what he described as "the dark poetry" of *Winesburg, Ohio.* At the age of seventeen he discovered *The Sun Also Rises,* and never lost his initial enthusiasm for "the virility of a style where implication reigned; I delighted in the rakishness of the great unsaid."

Wallant's essential education, then, was self-education, and with it came self-awareness—slowly at first, and then with a lyric rush that would do credit to any of his own "transformed" heroes. If the story of his life seems commonplace, one is struck by his ability to decipher quotidian codes, to transform a casual experience into an epiphanic moment. His brief job as a plumber's assistant or a pharmacist's delivery boy; the hours he spent in a relative's Harlem pawnshop; the loneliness of his bereaved father-in-law: all would be transformed into dense narrative structures. As Wallant's editor, Dan Wickenden, once remarked, "Like all born writers, he was a kind of sponge, soaking up experience, other people's as well as his own, constantly observing, with a remarkably penetrating eye, and imaginatively embroidering on what he observed."

In the final months of the Second World War, Wallant served as a gunner's mate in the European Theater of Operations. By the time of his discharge in 1946, he was determined to be an artist and enrolled at the Pratt Institute. In 1947 he married Joyce Fromkin, whom he had known since childhood, and in 1948 they moved to Brooklyn. Although he nurtured loftier ambitions, Wallant concentrated on commercial art and graduated from Pratt in 1950 into the blossoming postwar world of American advertising. He was almost immediately employed by the L. W. Frohlich Agency, and in 1957 moved on to McCann Erikson, where he was art director for (among others) the prestigious Westinghouse account. It was, in a modest way, a successful professional career, but it left Wallant deeply dissatisfied. He continued to paint and draw, but the visual arts failed to give him the satisfaction he found in literature—the power "of recording dreams, of escaping into other bodies and things." Consequently, in 1950 he enrolled at the New School for Social Research, where he studied creative writing with Charles Glicksberg and Don Wolfe. Under their guidance he produced a group of short stories and a clumsy but vigorous novel entitled *Tarzan's Cottage*—most of the writing done in longhand at a small kitchen table after a full day's work at the agency.

Wallant began submitting novels to publishers in the late 1950s—first *Tarzan's Cottage* and then *The Odyssey of a Middleman,* both of which were promptly rejected. The third book, *A Scattering on the Dark,* was accepted by Harcourt, Brace within twenty-four hours of its first reading and published in 1960 as *The Human Season.* Like most first novels, it received few reviews, but many of those were enthusiastic, and though sales were small, the book created a certain underground reputation for Wallant, thus assuring considerable attention for his next novel, *The Pawnbroker,* when it appeared in 1961. *The Human Season* won the Harry and Ethel Daroff Memorial Fiction Award as the best novel of the year on a Jewish theme; *The Pawnbroker* was nominated for the National Book Award, and movie rights were sold to Sidney Lumet. The career that had begun so modestly, tentatively, now seemed brilliantly launched. In 1960 Wallant attended the Breadloaf Writers Conference, where he seems to have been universally liked by his colleagues—though some were puzzled that he found no difficulty in reconciling his commercial and literary careers, or that he showed so few of the "mannerisms" of a writer.

In fact, Wallant was having increasing difficulty in reconciling his workaday life with the after-hours discipline of writing. Adding to the complications was his devotion for his three children—Scott, born 1952; Leslie, born 1954; and Kim, born 1957. Perhaps because he himself had been raised as a fatherless child, he wished to give his own children all the strength and assurance of a father's love; and perhaps because the household in which he had been raised was nonreligious, and he himself never Bar Mitzvahed, he insisted on the children being brought up in the Reformed Jewish faith. Again and again, as he sits at the kitchen table in New Rochelle, and later in Norwalk, his notes record the conflict between the voices of his children and the voices of the characters he is struggling to create.

The modest but solid success which greeted his first two novels seemed to promise a resolution to such conflicts, and in 1962, when he received a Guggenheim Fellowship, Wallant resigned his job at McCann Erikson with the idea of visiting Europe and returning home to be a full-time professional writer. For three months he traveled abroad. Joyce joined him in Italy, and when she returned to the children Wallant continued on to Spain. The brief European adventure almost immediately began taking shape in a brilliantly comic novel entitled *Tannenbaum's Journey*. Meanwhile, there were two other novels *(The Tenants of Moonbloom* and *The Children at the Gate)* to be completed, and Wallant took a room for himself in New York, where for the first time he had a retreat devoted entirely to his art. He was exhilarated by the European experience, by the new sense of craft that animated his work, and yet he was pale and tired, and complained of a persistent sore throat. Two complete medical checkups failed to reveal any physical problem, but quite suddenly one night he was stricken with what at first appeared to be an acute virus infection and lapsed immediately into a coma; he died one week later, on December 5, 1962, of an aneurism of the brain.

Wallant's early death led some commentators to find autobiographical allusions, a foreboding of death, in his hospital novel, *The Children at the Gate*. In fact, despite the tiredness he experienced in the last weeks of his life, friends remember him as being "alive to the tips of his fingers." He was, as ever, affable, genial, full of humor and a zest for living. Above all, he radiated a contagious enthusiasm for his new literary projects, for the vocation he now embraced with such passionate dedication.

CHAPTER 2

The Apprenticeship

I Fathers and Sons

NOTING that his four remarkably accomplished novels were produced within less than four years, commentators on Wallant's career have understandably stressed the naturalness and spontaneity of his talent. To be sure, the development of his narrative skills was, after some false starts, swift and self-assured, but the four novels and three short stories which found their way into print represent less than half of Wallant's literary production. Furthermore, both the published and the unpublished novels often exist in three or four distinct manuscript versions. For a man who held down a demanding, full-time job in advertising and who took with consistent seriousness his obligations as a father, the rate of production was truly prodigious. Wallant worked hard at his fiction, and he tirelessly revised all his works; if he strikes the reader as a "natural," such naturalness is the effect of a calculated and increasingly disciplined art, for there is little in the early writings to suggest more than the most pedestrian kind of talent. Still, these unpublished works, together with the three short stories Wallant published early in his writing career, are instructive for the student of *The Human Season, The Pawnbroker, The Children at the Gate,* and *The Tenants of Moonbloom.* First, they reveal a great deal about the author's methods. Variant drafts of individual works do not represent simple refinements or elaborations of the original treatment. Before *The Tenants of Moonbloom* Wallant's practice was to write a novel or story in full, then to rewrite it entirely from a new point of view. His first novel, for example, exists in four distinct versions, and there are three extant drafts of the late novel, *The Children at the Gate.* Normally, Wallant would retain the essential outlines of his plot,

19

but imagery, mood, theme, and point of view might be radically altered. The process itself is reminiscent of the kind of self-disciplining, self-critical exercise often used in creative-writing classes, and it taught him, no doubt, a great deal about his craft. For each variant of each work, Wallant would prepare a detailed "chapter outline" which indicated not only physical action and setting but often, as well, the response he wished to evoke through particular episodes. Only late in his career, with ever-increasing confidence in his own skills, did Wallant abandon the outline technique and begin to compose his work directly.

The apprentice writings are of further interest because of the author's tendency to cannibalize his own work. A single scene in an early, unpublished novel becomes the germ for another, entirely different novel. A character or episode may well reoccur in several unrelated works. Gradually, too, through the early writings we can observe Wallant isolating the themes and situations that were to distinguish his published novels. His heroes are often fatherless; they tend toward passive, even apathetic, states; surrogate fathers and brothers abound; and Wallant's own hometown of New Haven, Connecticut, forms the stable, traditionally oriented setting against which their disoriented experiences are set in dramatic relief.

II *"Fight Night"*

Before departing for Europe in 1962, Wallant destroyed many of his early manuscripts. "Fight Night," a story written for Don Wolfe's creative-writing course at the New School, survives as the earliest example of his fiction.[1] It is an embarrassingly naive little tale, scarcely more than an anecdote, about a thirty-seven-year-old black prizefighter preparing for a match. Despite his age, the boxer still dreams of winning the heavyweight championship; the fight, however, ends in a knockout victory for his opponent. Scarcely a phrase in the story suggests even the most modest claim to talent, and the distance traveled from this stilted, self-conscious study of the boxer to Wallant's compassionate, finely modulated portrait of Del Rio, the fastidious prizefighter in *The Tenants of Moonbloom,* can only be reckoned in creative light years. While Wallant's prose was never entirely free of embarrassingly poetic metaphor and excessive ornamentation, it was never again so riddled with cliché or wreathed in purple prose. The following sentences are unhappily representative of the general quality of the work: "Riding up in the elevator he was washed by a wave of weariness that made him impatient to get to his room." "His muscles were like gelatin, his insides fluttery and weak." ". . . he felt the old familiar knot in his stomach, small and cold." "Suddenly the dark figure sagged as if a great doll, its mechanism unwound, was returning to its inert unlife." In the sort of dream-reminiscence Wallant was to use successfully in *The Human Season*, his nameless boxer drifts off to sleep: "Warm, silky sand sifting coolly through his brown fingers powdering their darkness, made clouds as it fell through sunlight on the clothes line momma's dresses cast flat wiggly shadows on the ground the air was hot with droning stillness. . . . "

III *"The Man Who Made a Nice Appearance"*

Under the guidance of Don Wolfe, Wallant quickly pruned his language of many of these more poetic excesses. In another story written for his creative-writing class, Wallant described a young boy named Robert who awakens in fear one night to realize that both of his parents have left the house. Later, the father returns and the boy learns that his mother has died of a heart attack. He is raised by a black woman, and has only the dimmest, most detached relationship to his silent father. Later in his life, an unexpected moment of violence earns Robert the admiration of his young friends and eventually leads to his marriage, but on his wedding night he suddenly and inexplicably feels estranged from his bride and is unable to speak to her. He runs away and finds a new job as a clothing salesman in a distant city; his life is an empty, passionless routine, and as he grows older he looks forward only to death. In this original form, Wallant's story seems affected and pointless; Robert's character is not so much explored and revealed as manipulated by the author and woodenly demonstrated in a series of set, static scenes. With Don Wolfe's assistance, the story was thoroughly revised, and while the narrative machinery of the final version published in *New Voices* still creaks rather ominously, it shows considerable refinement in technique.

"The Man Who Made a Nice Appearance" has interesting parallels to Melville's *Bartleby the Scrivener*. Robert is one of

Wallant's remote, emotionally anaesthetized young men, and there is at least a hint that the condition springs from the loveless relationship with his father. Like Bartleby, Robert consciously seeks an anonymous, routine job, and because he makes "a nice appearance," he enjoys modest success as a clothing salesman. But his appearance also leads his colleagues to expect human qualities which he does not possess, and when they attempt to appeal to those qualities, Robert becomes the man who "would prefer not to." Similarly, after a unique fit of anger causes him to attack a drunk who has shouted obscenities at him and his youthful friends, he begins to receive unexpected demands and confidences: "He found himself caught up in a driving energy that seemed not to be his own. More was demanded of him by his friends. He was consulted and convinced, respected for attitudes he wasn't aware of. They called him at odd hours and confided things to him that he had no understanding of. It seemed remarkable to him that he seemed to perform as they wished." One of the friends impressed by Robert's attack on the drunk is the young woman he marries; he courts her with the ritual gestures and set phrases he knows to be expected on such occasions, but still maintains his vague detachment. As the two stand before the minister on their wedding day, Robert's attention drifts to his father's "huge, gently folded hands," and he almost gives way to nostalgia for the boyhood he has left behind, but then "he ordered his mind into the neat and careful track it had worn smooth and comfortable." Later, after making love to his bride, he suddenly sees the futility of his efforts to conform to the pattern his peers have expected. His silence frightens his wife, and when she asks him why he does not speak, he replies, simply, "What is there to say?"

Wandering through strange cities, through a series of jobs as a clothing salesman, Robert eventually finds his Bartlebylike place in the symbolic firm of "Icer and Calmer," a rented room "on a quiet, slowly dying street," and lives his life with "liquid anonymity." ("He rose in the morning, cleaned his body thoroughly and went to work in the soft-carpeted hush of the store. He ate his meals with no special hungers and went back to the spartan comfort of his room in the evening.") Like so many of Wallant's later heroes, Robert experiences "no more abrasion of pain than a shining, water-scrubbed rock in a rushing stream," though in an image to be repeated in the description of Norman

Moonbloom's isolation, he begins to fear that he is after all protected from the awful emptiness of life only by "a thin and membranous covering." At the conclusion of the story, Robert lies on his bed yearning for death. While Robert's anomie prefigures that of Wallant's later heroes, theirs will be broken by some shock of recognition, some blow to the spirit's sleep which will permit them to rejoin the world. In anticipation of another of his central themes, Wallant at least implies that Robert's hopeless condition results from a failure of nurture—that if he had only received from his own father some of the care he lavished on his garden, the boy's emotional life might have been made whole: "He would watch the great hands of the man, studying the careful, nurturing caress of the frail plants as though some key to his own solitude could be there. Large and pale they flexed and hovered in the darkening yard and vaguely, deep under the layers of memory, he felt a stirring as though he recalled a time when those hands had held him in infinite comfort."

IV *"Robert"*

In a further, unrelated story about a boy named Robert, the father-son theme is even more explicitly developed. An invalid father, crippled by arthritis, promises someday to tell his son a secret that will make him "king of the world." Robert worships this twisted, cynical father, and they are nearly constant companions, for his mother works as a milliner, his maiden aunts as bookkeepers, and his grandfather runs a small grocery store. The invalid father remains at home with the boy and his aged grandmother. Wallant's portrait of childhood here is nostalgic and sentimental; Robert and his friends play in the grape arbor, chase fireflies, go on outings to the beach with his father: "He and Lenore splashed and made sandcastles and he cut his foot on a clamshell. Later they rode on the flying horses and his was gold. On the way back they were sleepy and silly and the sky was gold while the earth was deep blue." Such nostalgic experiences soon come to an end, however. Robert's grandfather dies and the following winter the grandmother goes blind; the aunt dies in the spring, the father becomes bedridden, and the mother increasingly worn and haggard as she struggles to support the family. Finally Robert's father calls him to his bedside to give

him the long-promised secret, in a scene that anticipates the
distinctive voice, the sure command of dialogue, that would mark
Wallant's mature works:

"I'm going to die very soon. No, that's all right, there's no point to me
anymore anyhow. But you, you. Listen, it doesn't have to be like this. It
can be very different for you. A man needs a big deal, that's what he
needs. No little grocery store, no millinery shop, no bookkeeping. A big,
big deal. And I've studied it and studied it and I know what direction
you should take."
   A trolley went by with a melancholy iron roar. The crickets
chattered and rang and a smell of grape and flowers came in the
window along with the odor of wet ashes. They breathed at each other
fiercely, their eyes clawing at each other with an intensity that made it
seem like hatred. He's going to die, they'll all leave me. He strained for
the rescue of the secret.
   "Land." His father closed his mouth on the word. Slowly he nodded it
into his son. "Yes, real estate. Let me tell you about it. Sit down, there
on the bed. Go on, what I have isn't catching. Yes, that's it. Good. See, I
can touch your hand when I feel like it. Fine. All right now. . . . "

Later, lying awake in his own bed, Robert thinks of real estate as
some vague topic "that men talked about over cigars, grubby,
dull," and feels that his father has somehow violated the secret.
Yet gradually the father's feverish excitement infects the boy; he
feels a kingdom awaits him, and that dream becomes his private
antidote to the cautiously rational mentality of the family after
his father dies. Dramatically, Wallant's untitled story is well
conceived, and as an ironic comment on the "heritage" a father
passes to his son, it is central to the development of his later
novelistic vision. Nonetheless, it remains a two-dimensional
exercise; the author asserts where he should demonstrate, and is
too conscious of his central theme to permit the characters to
exist in their own right.

V   *"Fathers"*

A later story entitled "Fathers," though equally contrived,
shows considerably more sophistication in the presentation of
character, and its extensive revisions suggest it had particular
value for the author. The story is set in the intensive-care unit of
a metropolitan hospital—actually, a kind of "isolation ward" with
patients separated by glass panels so that the drama at one

bedside is visible at the next. Two sons come there to visit their fathers. One, Martin Mynder, has followed this routine for three years; the other, Freddie Bussman, is the son of a new patient with a "gaunt, handsome face and the coldly beautiful eyes of an ascetic or a hero." Freddie's father is dying of tuberculosis, and his son sees more of him now than ever before, for the boy had lived with his grandparents while his mother nursed the sick man in an apartment some blocks away. Though weak and small, Freddie has dreams of heroism inspired by tales of his own father's once violent, passionate life as an army officer: "Now, in the waning light, you could see by the way he gazed at the gaunt face on the pillow, how deep was the wound of his desire for emulation." His father, on the other hand, angered by the disease that is slowly killing him, "let his eyes fall on his son with only a remote expression of curiosity shading his exasperation."

In contrast to Freddie, Martin Mynder is a tough, unsentimental young man; his job in a drugstore links him to the cynical Angelo DeMarco in *The Children at the Gate*. Though the two sons never meet, a kind of competitiveness develops between them as they share, through the glass wall, these visits with their dying fathers. In a sense, the fathers and sons are mis-matched. Robert Bussman's injunction to his son would seem better addressed to Martin Mynder: "Don't you dare to live safely! Don't listen to them, to mother and grandma, do you hear. Walk the high wires, *burn,* boy, *burn!* Don't worry about dying. It doesn't matter at all. The dead don't even exist!" In the grim, anticipatory quiet that follows this outburst, Freddie realizes he will never be like his father: "He would tread no high wires nor stand astride things he had conquered, but instead he would always lay down with spread arms to say 'Uncle' or any other litany required in order to live out his life of beige and soft gray. And he began to grieve for that even before his choice was irrevocable." When the dying father calls Freddie to his bedside, the grandmother, fearful of possible contagion, holds the boy back, and he surrenders easily to her restraint. Later, at the burial of Martin Mynder's father, when the rabbi asks the man's Hebrew name and no one knows it, his son trembles with anger: "A terrible life had been lived in pain and betrayal and grief and yet no one knew the man's name!" At this moment the street-toughened boy weeps and then rages against the meek father's surrender to fate, declaring his own "war on life." The two sons of dying fathers have never met, and the last sentence of the story seems gratuitous, almost nonsensical: "The two boys never saw each other again except in dreams." Despite the story's arch contrivance, its overloaded parallels and contrasts, it offers a moving variation on Wallant's theme of the critical relationship between fathers and sons, and many of the implications of the story would be dramatically and far more persuasively explored in *The Children at the Gate*. Freddie Bussman appears again as the child hero of Wallant's unpublished novel *Tarzan's Cottage*, and Martin Mynder as the failed middle-aged artist in *Odyssey of a Middleman*.

VI   *"The Days to Come"*

Partly because its dramatic conception is more distilled and its action concentrated within a shorter time span, "The Days to Come" is a more successful treatment of the death of a father than the Mynder-Bussman story. Here a man named Marty is seen on the day following his father's funeral as he opens up the clothing store where they once worked together. As the figures of various neighborhood characters move through the shop offering their condolences, one is reminded of the technique of *The Pawnbroker*. Near the conclusion of the story a working-class mother comes to the store to buy shoes for her child; she rejects the more expensive merchandise, and when Marty fits cheap shoes on the child she accuses him of selling inferior merchandise. He explodes,

"It's a good store, we don't sell crap, it's my father's store . . . my father never sold crap," he screamed, his face red and fierce, "you shut up your filth," he sobbed, the tears flooding his fat stubbled face. "My father's store, my father . . . ," he sat on the floor, his hands over his face, his body shaking.

Rejecting all attempts to pacify him, the hero ultimately finds comfort by accepting the simple rhythm of the store itself, the scene of so many years of collaboration with his dead father.

VII   *"I Held Back My Hand"*

In Wallant's two posthumously published novels, *The Children at the Gate* and *The Tenants of Moonbloom*, the theme of the craving for paternal recognition is submerged beneath that of fraternal relationships. In "I Held Back My Hand," as in "Fathers," the implied fraternity is denied. The narrator of the story is haunted by memories of Max Faibling, a moody, ugly, excitable boy whom he had known in his school days. With something of Sammy Cahan's *spieling* ways, Max resembles "a great bird, frightful and delicate, his eyes stabbing in every direction, his mouth a thin, pink line under the beak of nose." Even Max's games resemble Sammy's tragic clowning in *The Children at the Gate:*

In Larry's backyard, among the grape arbors and weedy clumps of grass, he created games of make believe in which he was always the victim: a spear-pierced explorer or a mortally wounded duellist, he writhed horribly, joyfully in the death throes, a sumac sword held against his chest, his face, blanched and grim with approaching death. "I die," he screamed, "that they may live."

Clearly a victim of parental neglect, Max appeals to the narrator through his marvelously theatrical gestures and stories, and for a time they become friends. Later, with the courting and partying of adolescence having become far more important than contact with the awkward, aggressive Max, the narrator abandons him, only years later to be requested by school authorities to visit the friendless young man in hospital, where he is recovering from attempted suicide. This confrontation with the gaunt figure of Max and with his own denial of friendship causes the narrator intense pain: "Max looked, for the first time, like an ugly, weeping child, as if, for that brief moment, the tears had washed away the old man face. I felt a deep impulse to clutch his monstrous head tight against my body, to kiss his parched lips, to hold him deeply, in love, as I would my own child." But Max rejects this guilty comforter, who leaves him in a rush of fear and shame. "I Held Back My Hand" was, like "The Man Who Made a Nice Appearance," polished and refined under the guidance of the New School's Don Wolfe before being included in one of the *New Voices* volumes he edited. It was the first of Wallant's published stories, Max Faibling the first of his improbable Christ figures, and it thus suggests how early he was experimenting with the kinds of human confrontations that characterize the later novels.

VIII   *"Life is a Fountain"*

Wallant's most ambitious story, "Life Is a Fountain," was obviously important to him, for extensive notes on the piece are among his papers, as well as two different manuscript versions, both extensively revised. The revisions show an increasing sense of craft, a willingness to allow the story to tell itself without the obtrusive stylistic manipulations that spoil most of the early work, and without the cumbersome subplot Wallant originally conceived.[2] In the first version of the story, the opening sentence reads, "There seemed something sadly conclusive about the fact that the train car was old and shabby and that the heat wasn't working." In the final revision, the opening words are pruned away to leave the more explicit statement that "The train car was old and shabby and the heat wasn't working." Wallant was at last learning to curb some of his own excesses, but all his careful editing could not save the story, which seems a direct echo of F. Scott Fitzgerald, and clearly needed Fitzgerald's lighter touch to succeed at all.

Gene, the central character and observing consciousness of the story, is returning to his old hometown of New Haven for the first time since his father's funeral there four years before. He thinks of his own parents as having existed together in bondage, not in matrimony, and his sour attitude toward marriage seems confirmed by all his married friends. He imagines that this visit to New Haven will eliminate the final exception to this rule—Steve and Fran Ehrlich, who had always seemed "impossibly beautiful," and like fairy-tale characters in their love for each other. Through the years and despite the demands of children, hobbies, professional advancement, they have always maintained their good looks, and Gene is surprised to note "a whining querulous note" in Fran's voice when she telephones to ask him to visit. He arrives at a woodsy suburban house full of the warm insignia of domesticity, and for a moment imagines that he was wrong to think this marriage would have gone sour too. Then he finds Steve grown fat, his wife aged and ill-looking. Still, they manage to convey the image of a happy family: "It was all like one of those Kodak, full-color panoramas in Grand Central: the perfect-setting living room with its bright fire, the blonde mother in her suburban tweed and cashmere, the model-like unpimpled children, the father leaning with virile ease against the fireplace with a drink in his hand. . . ." The resemblance to a Fitzgerald tableau is one that even the wife in the story can recognize: "You used to say we were too perfect, like F. Scott Fitzgerald characters only with our feet safely on the ground."

Fran has summoned her old friend because of concern about her husband. During her own acute illness with rheumatic fever, she had had to abstain from sexual relations, and because Fran now fears that Steve has found another woman, she persuades her old friend to follow the husband during one of his late evenings in town. Steve goes to a restaurant where, Gene presumes, he will have a rendezvous with a woman, and his face is suffused with passion as he sits down to order a drink and then an enormous meal on which he gorges himself; gluttony, it turns out, is his sole and solitary compensation for a sexless marriage. The triumph Gene had felt in learning that this "one gaping hole in his defense of bachelorhood" had closed turns to self-pity. He knows the "harsh, iron taste of impoverishment and his own loneliness seems like a far corridor leading off to an emptiness so terrible it will drive him mad." When he reports his discovery to Fran and claims to be both disgusted and bewildered by it, she attempts to explain by comparing her love for her husband to "a snowball that grows as it rolls down a hill. . . ."

"Oh, Jesus Christ," Gene muttered exasperatedly as he fixed his eyes on a cobweb in the corner of the phone booth.

"It picks up all kinds of dirt, bits of filth and sharp branches, and pieces of glass and rough stones. It's dangerous, it . . . well, it can kill you. It isn't white and clean and perfect like when it was new. But it's bigger, Gene, it's so much *bigger* . . ."

Gene hung up on her soft, peaceful crying and walked out of the drugstore, into the cold winter night of the city. He was stunned and felt as though a joke had been played on him.

But as he looked up at the stars framed by the ancient landscape of his childhood, he couldn't, for the life of him, understand the punch line. Or know for sure how long ago the joke had been perpetrated.

The terrors of a loveless life insinuate themselves into all of Wallant's later writings, but in "Life Is a Fountain" the contrast between Gene, the character insulated against love, and Fran and Steve, star-crossed lovers acting out a black comedy of love that nonetheless sustains them, is too static to engage the reader at any significant level. Despite occasional passages in which

Wallant demonstrates his growing control of language, the story seems little more than an embroidered anecdote. Having created, now, a minor gallery of unloved, unloving, lonely men, Wallant was ready to chronicle the transfigurations that would cancel loneliness and link his heroes to the community of man.

IX *The Willy Novels*

Wallant's shorter fiction shows little talent for conceiving and dramatizing those metaphoric situations, recognitions, revelations that characterize the short story at its best. His imagination seemed to work novelistically, seeing fictional experience in terms of more extended actions, more sprawling casts of characters, than the shorter form could contain. Hence, with few exceptions, the short stories seem melodramatic and clumsily contrived. The early novels are not free of such weaknesses, but they show remarkable assurance in building character.

What Wallant himself thought of as "The Willy Novels" are all concerned with a young boy whose mother has died of diabetes and who grows up with his father and his sister Min. The first two versions of the book, entitled *Willy*, feature a shy young boy who becomes increasingly dissatisfied with life as he grows older. Fat and rather repulsive, he is excluded from the games of other children, and later becomes a manual laborer in a factory, where he need engage neither his heart nor his mind. When he kisses a girl for the first time at a New Year's party and is clearly overwhelmed by the experience, his colleagues decide to take him to visit a whore. Willy desperately wants the experience to be beautiful. When he finds it merely sordid, he savagely beats the woman. His sister's wedding makes him feel even more excluded, like "an intruder on some intimacy." He gets drunk, passes out in the rain, and contracts pneumonia. When he is well again, Willy decides to go away—first to Cleveland, where he works as a dishwasher, then to Detroit and Chicago, always roaming after some vague goal he cannot articulate. He discovers in this time the perfect solitary entertainment of reading, but it makes him even more restless. On impulse, he tries to telephone his father, only to have the phone answered by a cleaning lady who does not know him, and in despair he wanders for three years throughout America before returning home again.

This basic structure remains constant in the first two versions of the novel, but there are remarkable differences in Wallant's handling of these modest materials. In the first Willy novel one has a literal, pedestrian "recording" of childhood, of encounters with the adult world and with violence, of a bruising adolescence and aimless adulthood. The novel, set largely in the 1930s, has little dialogue and relates events from an entirely external point of view. In the second version, rich in imaginative invention, dialogue is extended, Willy's emotions are dramatized rather than merely described, and language itself is more pointed and evocative. Willy Chain is no longer merely labeled as a shy child but revealed as someone who, after being beaten up by other children, withdraws "deep into that thick cave of his body." The novel is enriched with incident—a love affair with a fat, blowsy blonde in the boardinghouse where Willy lives after leaving home and Huck Finnish adventures with two hoboes with whom he travels in the West, shoplifting food and sleeping under railway bridges. Eventually Willy gets work as a movie extra, chiefly because of his vast bulk, and falls in love with a bit actress who, like him, is Jewish. The Hollywood sections of the novel are well imagined, the shabby glamour thoroughly convincing. When Willy's girlfriend begins to win modest success with speaking parts, he finds himself jealous and resentful, and once more takes to the road. Among his new companions is an old man who gives him a ride; the two become friends, and when the man dies he takes the body to St. Louis for burial.

In St. Louis, Willy meets a bitter black man named Singer, who sits on the fire escape of the boardinghouse where he and Willy live and sings Italian arias. Singer is one of Wallant's first successful minor characters—the kind of fully fleshed, utterly distinctive figure with which he would so graphically and memorably populate the world of *The Pawnbroker* and *The Tenants of Moonbloom*. The two men become constant companions, and Willy feels betrayed when he comes home one day to discover Singer in a rage, having destroyed all his opera records, wrecked the room, and cut himself with a razor. Overcome by his feeling of responsibility for the angry black, Willy cries out in a line that echoes throughout Wallant's later works, "What am I, a saint or something?" As though to confirm this role, Singer begins to test his white friend—making scenes in public, playing dangerous jokes, breaking a grocery-store window, and finally raping a woman. Willy remains true and helps Singer escape, only to be subjected to further and ever more strenuous tests of his loyalty. Despite Singer's occasional bursts of madness, he and Willy manage to make a kind of home together on Chicago's South Side—not unlike the bizarre but sustaining domestic relations of Ratso Rizzo and Joe Buck in James Leo Herlihy's *Midnight Cowboy.* Through their experiences together Willy slowly develops a kind of visionary insight. When the war comes, Willy earns a large salary working in a war plant, but Singer has become too unstable to work at all. Willy wonders why he remains, but submits to another vigil with the hysterical black man. Late at night, Willy falls exhaustedly to sleep and awakens to find that Singer has killed himself by jumping from the window.

Tempered by his bizarre adventures, Willy returns home at the age of thirty-two and is astonished that, despite so many physical changes, everything seems uncannily the same as when he was a boy there. His widowed sister has two sons, and with one of them, Harry, he develops a strong, protective relationship. When the older nephew, Paul, contracts polio, Willy is angered by the burden of invalidism that Harry is forced to assume. Everywhere he turns he meets only defeated men and women, and he begins to record their faces with a cheap box camera, thinking of his snapshots as "visions, insights," and always searching for the one photograph that will express his own sense of life. Some of it, at least, he articulates for himself at the funeral of his nephew Paul, when a friend attempts to console him: "They should mourn about their lives. This takes care of itself." Such attitudes are incomprehensible to his family, and they draw away from him in horror. At the age of forty Willy tries to start a new life in marriage, but though his wife weaves "a web of domesticity around him," the marriage breaks up.

On a hot August day Willy suddenly has the feeling that he will get the photograph he has so long sought. He spends the day taking pictures, drinking, enjoying the images and sounds of the city, and then injures himself when he falls through a plate-glass window. Harry and a friend find Willy sitting in a stupor on the green in New Haven, and when they lead him home Min recognizes that he is seriously ill. He is put to bed in the room he had occupied as a child, but the next morning gets up to go to work, collapses near the schoolyard, and dies. As he loses consciousness he looks up to see "the camera inches away from where it had fallen. A piece of his own face was reflected in its unbroken lens." The concluding image gives Wallant the title for a later version of the Willy novel— *The Ground Glass View.* The lovingly paternal relationship with Harry leads, in turn, to a manuscript entitled *Willy and Harold,* in which Willy's adventures are told from Harry's point of view. Ultimately, Wallant also produced a short story, which exists in several versions, about the two nephews. His fascination with the Chain family was to be matched later by his sagas of the Gimple family.

The flaws of the Willy novels are obvious even from a condensed description of their plots. Fragmentary, episodic, loosely structured, and self-indulgent, they are vigorous but undisciplined works. Nonetheless, following the stilted first version of the novel Wallant showed an increasingly inventive narrative sense, and he sketched out relationships that were to be far more persuasively developed in his later writings. The friendship of Willy and Singer is taken up in the uneasy friendship of black and Jew in *View of a Marvelous City,* the first version of *The Children at the Gate,* and it has parallels, too, in the relationship between Sol Nazerman and his Puerto Rican assistant, Jesus Ortiz. Willy's awakening, his emergence from the cave of self, was to become Wallant's major theme, and his protective feelings for his young nephew once more stress the significance of paternal relationships in Wallant's world of orphans and outcasts.

X   Tarzan's Cottage

The Tarzan who lends his name to Wallant's second novel is no Edgar Rice Burroughs creation, though he has something of the original's vigor and masculine dignity. A hotelkeeper on the Connecticut shore, he opens his rambling cottage every summer to vacationers from New Haven, and in the summer of 1937 his guests include the Bussman family, Joe and Tilly Marx and their retarded daughter, and Harry Bodien, who reappears in *The Human Season* as Joe Berman's assistant. The Bussmans—a tubercular father, his wife and son Freddie—are familiar figures in Wallant's writings; they not only appear by name in the short story "Fathers," but narrative details suggest identification with the family described in "Robert." Freddie—whose kinship to "Eddie" Wallant is always strong—lives with his grandparents while his mother nurses his invalid father Martin. A city boy, young Freddie is thrilled by the strange smells of the cottage and the sea and finds surrogate fathers both in the energetic Tarzan and in a retiring, rather cynical bill-collector named Theodore Middleman. *Tarzan's Cottage* is thematically a conventional story of adolescent initiation in which a young boy comes slowly to terms with his own identity: "In the reality of time and place he found himself briefly able to transcend his natural physique of trepidation and uncertainty. A part of him he had never seen before asserted a powerful joy."

All who come to Tarzan's Cottage are, in a sense, cripples—the invalid Martin Bussman, the young retarded girl most obviously so, but even Freddie is in a sense crippled because he has been so rigorously sheltered from life (and death) by his adoring, indulgent grandparents. From a dead fish rotting on the beach to the strangulation of the idiot girl Reba, the summer will bring lessons about death, but also abundant evidence of life in the bounty and the festive mood provided by Louis B. ("Tarzan") Riverman.

At home, eating was only "a function of subdued nourishment," but here

there was a festivity in the very size and variety of crowding foods. The steam came up to soften the faces of the people, to lave them with the smells of yellow corn, of umber meats and the green, jewelry freshness of lettuce and celery. Great bloody wedges of tomato clashed with the maroon succulence of tiny beets. Bread was there in brown and white beside the awkward hugeness of yellow tub butter. In the center, on a huge revolving stand, the condiments stood proud as generals reviewing the teeming field. . . .

Sated by this bounty, the small community is joined together by laughter and by the fierce energy of their host. Freddie's own rite of passage into the bounty and terror of life will be symbolized in the novel by his learning to swim, and by the necessity of choosing between two very different teachers—the bearish Tarzan or the isolated Middleman. Without a father who could teach him such things, and continuously sheltered by his cautious grandparents, Freddie has never learned to play ball, to ride a bicycle, to do anything physically challenging. While the adults debate about his instruction, Freddie is filled with terror:

"He thought of cramps and the terrible depths of the ocean as he had learned of them from the echo of his grandparents' old warnings. Suddenly he was aware of the awfulness of change. . . ."

Freddie's initiation is played out against the background of news of rising conflict in Europe and rumors of genocide in Germany. When Middleman takes Freddie fishing one night, they encounter a seaplane trying to land "tourists," Jewish refugees unable to enter the country legally. The subplot drags badly, though it also plays a major role in Freddie's education: he turns the Jews in out of a desire to do something "big and terrible" in his life, to show his strength. The act destroys the sense of community he has enjoyed, even though Tarzan struggles yet harder to buoy the group up. Despite their outspoken condemnation of Freddie's action, the other summer guests begin to confide their secrets to the boy, as though his outrageous act has persuaded them of his special powers. But the novel has clearly gotten out of control, and all Wallant's efforts to mend and revise it are unsuccessful. He heaps episode upon episode to revive the novel's flagging rhythm: a wrestling match between Tarzan and an Italian friend (recreated for *The Human Season*), a competition in which Tarzan and Freddie's father walk on burning coals, and, on the last day of summer, Freddie's heroic swim to the big rock in the bay. In his head Freddie has heard Middleman's voice throughout this strenuous ordeal, and Middleman is, ultimately, the superior teacher. Disfigured in the war, disillusioned by life, he is one of Wallant's isolatoes, but with an insight into the boy's conflicted personality that neither Tarzan nor Martin Bussman possesses. Freddie finally lies exhausted on the rock that was his goal, and it is Middleman who rows out to bring him home. This resolution of the father-child theme is immediately and grotesquely undercut when Joe Marx strangles his retarded daughter.

After their return to New Haven, the Bussmans once more live together as a family, but as his illness worsens, Martin Bussman's nihilism grows more bitter, and Freddie is enervated by the constant rancors and wranglings of the adult world. On Armistice Day a parade passes the house, and Freddie watches his friend Tarzan march proudly by with a bright orange zinnia in his mouth. The boy stands on the sidewalk, while his father watches

from the window above, propped up in his bed. There is, in this
consciously climactic scene, much meeting of eyes, much implied
mystical communing, but it fails to resolve the complex welter of
themes and counterthemes, conflicts, parallels, and contrasts
Wallant has heaped on the story. Martin Bussmann dies at
Christmas, and Freddie must now learn to apply the lessons he
learned at Tarzan's Cottage.

XI   Odyssey of a Middleman

Like all of Wallant's novels, *Odyssey of a Middleman* went
through several working drafts, and though all of them fail, the
final draft is far more finished, more professional, than any of his
earlier efforts. The story describes a middle-aged man, Martin
Mynder, who despite the similarity in names bears only
occasional resemblances to the Martin Mynder of "Fathers." As
the novel opens, Martin is going home to New Haven, having
failed at making a career as a painter, with the intention of using
money left him by his brother Sidney to buy part interest in a
pharmacy. Recalling now his earlier life, Martin typically
remarks, "I never knew my father," who had gone into a rest
home when his son was nine, and died there of multiple sclerosis.
The Mynders are truly middlemen—"neither rich nor poor,
beautiful nor ugly, brilliant nor dull, neither Saint nor good, lusty
Sinner."[3] The father, a landlord who refused to raise the rents on
his black tenants despite spiraling costs, passes his philosophy on
to his son: "He thought that no one should inflict pain on another
living creature. No provocation excused it for him so he had lived
his life in a terrible agony, for of course, we all know that life isn't
lived that way. . . . Sometime, very early in his life in a Russian
village, he had interpreted the laws of God all wrong and he had
been forced to live in the wrong world ever after."
    Martin inherits his father's "gentle sort of cowardice," and a
tendency to accept unquestioningly whatever destiny presents
him. In this neutral, undramatic world, his first sense of tragedy
comes at his father's funeral when, in a scene directly transposed
from "Fathers," the rabbi asks the dead man's Hebrew name and
no one replies. "I felt pain I had never realized could exist. They
didn't know his name, his real name, I thought. He went through
a terrible life uncomplainingly, endured pain, betrayals, outrage,
fear, grief. And no one knows his name." Martin's childhood, as

Wallant recalls it, bears striking parallels to the author's own; perhaps the literalness of his source accounts for the flatness with which Martin's early years are recounted. At any rate, these episodes are the weakest in the novel. During the financially difficult Depression years, Martin takes various part-time jobs, meanwhile continuing to follow his passionate interest in drawing. One of those jobs gives us the first glimpse of the world that would become the setting for *The Children at the Gate:*

The Chapel Pharmacy stood on a corner facing two of New Haven's three big hospitals. Commercially, it was Lord of all it surveyed for its nearest competitor was, in Abe Moskowitz's own words, "A Swede with a goyisha cup who's no competition at all." We of the Chapel Pharmacy (I say "we" in deference to Abe who liked me to feel I was part of the business even at four dollars a week) had all the business from the nurses' home as well as the faithful patronage of the interns directly across the street.

Abe Moskowitz is a fatherly figure, giving the boy somewhat sententious advice about life but loving him for what he is—soft, sentimental, thorougly trusting.

One of Martin's duties at the pharmacy is to tour the nearby Catholic hospital to take orders from patients and nurses, and so he daily passes "the sweet disapproval of the Madonna's lamp-lit figure" in the lobby. Martin soon discovers a "friendly enemy" in an orderly named Genovese, with whom he occasionally sits eating pizza in the hospital solarium, and there is much "talismanic baiting" between the Catholic orderly and the Jewish errand boy. Though the relationship thus reverses the religious contrast of the later novel which it inspired, *The Children at the Gate*, it is in other ways strikingly similar. Genovese baits Martin in a way that compels him to consider his spiritual identity and tricks him into entering a dimly lighted alcove to take an order from a dead man. The rape which precipitates the climax of *The Children at the Gate* is here a well-hidden episode in the history of Martin's own family, for his sister was raped as a child by her uncle's friend; further, Martin learns that he has an older retarded brother, long since incarcerated in a state home. These secrets, plus "the constant assault of life and death, . . . birth and extinction" he witnesses in the hospital impel him toward his choice of profession; it comes to him as a revelation that the way to save himself from sordidness, madness, triviality, and death is to be an artist. In lines that also give us the source for Angelo Demarco's name in *The Children at the Gate*, he exults, "I'm saved, I'm saved. I can take anything those Mynders can dish out . . . Art, art, art. . . . Call me John Singer Leonardo da Angelo Mynder. . . ."

To earn money for art school, Martin works in a brickyard and on oyster boats, and even gets himself put onto a welter-weight fight card. After three years he goes to study in New York, where two of his first contacts at the Malcolm-Heters School are the black students Da Agostino and Singer. The latter, redrawn from the Willy novels, is "a small, ugly negro with a clever, malicious face which wore a constant, loveless life." Wallant's attempts to capture (or recapture from his own days at Pratt Institute) bohemian life in New York, with its affairs, loyalties, enthusiasms, and small successes, is a tedious exercise, but one ended by the arrival of Martin's draft notice. After infantry school and tank-training, he is assigned to a typing job in downtown Boston, and though he cannot type, his bookish senior officer seems happy to have a "sensitive" friend who can discuss ideas. Shipped out after Pearl Harbor, Martin experiences the war as "a series of nonsensical and pointless events, many drenched in horror . . . ," but he stumbles across his earlier life when he meets in an air-raid shelter his "long-lost Uncle Myron," whose friend had raped Martin's sister. A wound leads to one buttock being amputated, Candidelike, and to a brief flirtation, on the author's part, with black comedy. But the comedy is too fleeting, the seriousness of the novel too ponderous, its plot already inflexibly committed to the baroque. Returned to New York after the war, Martin rejects art school for a job in an advertising agency, falls in love with an actress, and tries to become, in his free time, a successful painter. In a line that seems nakedly autobiographical, Wallant has Martin reflect that "all day my mind seethed with formidable mysteries and it was fortunate that I had reduced the visual platitudes of the agency to a point where I could manage with roughly a third of my attention."

In the last chapters of the novel, Wallant struggles to bind up the dangling threads of his work. Martin has a modestly successful exhibition, marries his actress girl friend, collects his older brother from the asylum to attend their mother's funeral, separates from his wife, and finally inherits half of his brother Sidney's estate and returns to New Haven to buy out half of Abe Moskowitz's pharmacy. A failed artist himself, he nonetheless retains his deep feeling for the role of the artist in society:

I don't agree with Mendel Moskowitz or Abe that artists perform a secondary function, that they exist just to entertain after the real work is done. Quite to the contrary, I am more than ever convinced that they (the real ones, mind you, those willing and able to "Die to life") are our authentic Gods. For they teach us the inherent beauties, hold up to us the shifting aspects of meaning that drift like grains in all the flooding nonsense. All I know is that it *has* been beyond me. For a real artist everything is written into their contract with life.

Martin's sluggish existence establishes him as a "middleman," but so too does his ability to straddle the values of the workaday world and those of the world of art. A later Wallant hero, the kosher butcher Gimpel, has similar talents, but Wallant will be able to treat them with a good deal less of the somber self-consciousness he gives to Martin's story. What Wallant required to discipline his talents and channel his increasingly inventive imagination was to address himself to a far smaller canvas; like most fledgling writers he confused complexity of action for complexity of effect. The subject that would first reveal his mature powers as a writer he found very close to home, as he watched the painful struggles of his father-in-law to find some coherence and dignity in life following the death of his wife. Wallant tentatively entitled this new novel *A Scattering on the Dark*, and submitted it to Harcourt, Brace together with *The Odyssey of a Middleman*. Harcourt's editors rightly rejected the latter as a clumsy, amateurish work, but they accepted *A Scattering on the Dark* within twenty-four hours of its first reading and published it under the new title, *The Human Season*.

CHAPTER 3

The Human Season

I *Commonplace Griefs*

The Human Season is the most distilled and monochromatic of
Wallant's four published novels, and yet it presents us with an
image of the hero which remains consistent throughout the later
works. The relative simplicity of the novel's execution and its
compact dramatic structure make the hero's search for a viable,
authentic self particularly clear. Though its language sometimes
falters and its action verges toward melodrama, the work is a
resounding and often a deeply moving testimony to man's
spiritual resourcefulness. Its hero is the recognizable everyman
of twentieth-century fiction—undistinguished, undifferentiated
from the mass of middle-class laborers-fathers-providers; even
his griefs are commonplace. The title of Wallant's earlier
unpublished novel, *Odyssey of a Middleman,* would have suited
well this brief tale of a middle-aged man's unmanageable sorrow
following the death of his wife. A Russian Jew who immigrated to
America as a young boy, Joe Berman has fulfilled the minor
litanies of the American Dream. He has established his own
plumbing business, married a girl with the obligatory blonde,
American prettiness, owns his own modest home (on which the
mortgage is almost paid), and has fathered three children. His
only son is killed in the Second World War, bequeathing Berman
the guilt of their unspoken love, their unshared thoughts; and the
wife he cherished in his rough, bearish way has died three
months before the novel begins.

It is June 1956 when Berman returns to his empty house to
resume the rituals of daily life that he hopes will numb his grief.
Rejecting comfort and companionship, he nurtures his sorrow,
exacerbates it to a point where madness, suicide, or complete

40

despair seem his only options. This excessive, destructive grief is an assault on the religious faith of his boyhood—a reminder of how far this Americanized Jew has moved away from the sustaining fabric of his past. Perhaps more importantly, despair is one of the symptoms of that spiritual disease and dis-ease which threaten to culminate in the character's total isolation. Berman can see himself only as the pathetic victim of unjust forces, and thus begins his increasingly angry quarrel with the God who has betrayed him. So long as he can, Joblike, attribute his sufferings to a malevolent outside agent, Berman is able to delay the confrontation with self that is prerequisite to his rebirth into a new life of feeling and commitment, but the dialectic structure of the novel relentlessly nudges him toward that moment of self-recognition and redemption.

Considering its ultimate philosophical implications, the novel's structure is deceptively simple. Most of the eighteen chapters contain two sections; the first documents Berman's lonely, increasingly anguished vigil, while the second moves back in time to reveal some formative or traumatic episode of the past. The flashbacks not only deepen our understanding of the character; they also strip away, in their reverse progression into the past, the layers of habit and acculturation, to reveal the essential spirit of the young boy known, in a Russian village, as Yussel Berman. Like a compressed and particularly rigorous program of Freudian analysis, they probe each assumption, each uncertainty, each fear, laying bare the psyche of the character in a way that is often painful, but which also permits his spiritual rebirth. Viewed literally, these memories of time past are not flashbacks but dreams, which proceed backward in time from April 30, 1956, when Mary suffers her fatal stroke, to September 1907, when Berman was a boy of nine in Russia. The first half of each chapter thus represents Berman's increasingly dulled and narcotic waking life, while the second presents us through dreams with the increasingly vital experiences of the past. Occasionally Wallant links the waking life and the dream with some imagistic transition. The opening section of Chapter 11, for example, records Berman's lewd assault on his sweaty, alcoholic cleaning woman, and the feeling of abject revulsion their brief bout of lovemaking gives him. Driving her from the house, he stands in the hallway and begins to beat his head gently against the invisible pattern of the hallway wall, thumping it in the rhythm of prayer, but senselessly, not aware of what he was doing, in the manner that some babies put themselves to sleep. *Thump, thump thump, thump,* went his head against the dark wall. It was the only sound in the world (pp. 122–23).

The following dream section is set in the village of Dolmyk in Russia, on the December day in 1912 when Berman's father suffers a stroke and dies. The opening imagery of the section echoes Berman's present life: "Berman stood with his head against the glass, looking out at the huddled houses, cold and inward-facing in the winter afternoon" (p. 123). More important is the contrast between Berman's lust for an unwashed, bleach-blonde sexual athlete and the defining, comforting sense of disciple which the old religious laws had once given him: "Instinctively he loved the order his father had imposed, the shape and size the red-bearded man created with his laws" (p. 123).

   Such precise linkings of imagery and theme are not consistent in Wallant's treatment of past and present experience, yet throughout the novel runs a recurrent and increasingly anguished sense of the abandonment of the old values. On one level this can be read as the consequence of the relinquishing of a faith that was once nurturing and consoling—a faith slowly eroded by the new values and manners of a New World. Though they still lighted the Sabbath candles of the old faith, Joe and Mary were accustomed to sit together on Friday evenings, making "comforting complaints in the bright, labor-saving kitchen" (p. 17), and exchanging tidbits of gossip. As Wallant remarks, "Little remained of their Sabbath rituals, the special dinners they used to have in the beginning" (p. 17). The containers in which candles had been dutifully burned for Joe's and Mary's dead parents now serve as drinking glasses. The new rituals which have replaced the old exclude none of the joys of familiar intimacy, but they are more transient, more capricious than the traditional ones, as Joe will learn to his anguish after Mary dies. *The Human Season* holds no brief for a return to the old orthodoxy, and yet it mourns the passing of order and stability which Jewish Law once tendered, and Berman must acknowledge the spirit if not the letter of the ancient faith before he can be born to a new life. In this respect, *The Human Season* is the most self-consciously Jewish of Wallant's four published novels.

II   *The Denial of Nature*

Like the pawnbroker Sol Nazerman, Joe Berman is so warped away from the natural sources of feeling and emotion that he seems mechanical. Both make compulsive, ordering gestures that serve only to measure time, not to communicate any interior will, and they significantly hide their eyes behind thick, blurred glasses. The heavy-set, thick-handed Berman feels intimidated by reminders of his wife's delicacy and femininity, the work of her nurturing hands. Angered by the "feminine touch" of a plant his wife had cultivated, he flings it to the floor. Her soft, much-washed aprons seem to intimidate him, as do the gossamer of her hairnet, the soft pastel colors of her lotions and shampoos, the fragile mementos she had collected on their rare travels. In the powerful opening chapter of the novel, so densely redolent with grief, Joe moves like an alien through this feminine world, whose sole comforts are now those of cool, mechanical efficiency. When Mary is still alive, Wallant gives us a warm, intimate view of the "bright, labor-saving kitchen," and as Joe and Mary do the dishes together, the mechanical world itself seems pastorally transformed: "The refrigerator hummed, the water sloshed peacefully in the sink. Outside there was a lonely wind" (p. 18). But when Joe stands alone in the same room, he sees only its heartlessly functional aspects:

From the middle of the large, gleaming kitchen he surveyed the possible directions he could take. The refrigerator hummed its cool efficiency and the pilot light of the stove was a small blue eye in the growing dimness. He went to the wall switch, which had a flowered plate over it, and switched on the light. And standing there in all the chrome and formica and gleaming enamel, he created a moment of spiteful pleasure for himself.
"Buttons, switches—I'm a magician" (pp. 12-13).

What Wallant draws for us here is an agonizing portrait of the numbing, disorienting grief of an aging man. Berman's creation of such a hero at a time when America's chronic emphasis on youth was assuming new stridency was itself an act of novelistic courage. The classic American novel has focused on the "beardless youth" so tellingly anatomized by D. H. Lawrence. Only Saul Bellow, in *Mr. Sammler's Planet*, has created a comparably moving, finely drawn portrait of man near the end of his life. As a survivor of the concentration camps, a man literally

raised from the tomb, Sammler of course has direct correspondences to Sol Nazerman in *The Pawnbroker*, but Bellow's
description of the small domestic gestures by which the lonely
widower tries to make a life of dignity for himself amid the
rootlessness and violence of the American city often has striking
resemblances to Wallant's treatment of Berman. Bellow's careful
itemizing of Sammler's morning ritual, sipping grapefruit juice
from a container and grinding his own coffee, is a direct echo of
the spare but detailed language with which Wallant describes
Berman's morning rituals:

He put the kettle on to boil and sat down to wait for it. He brushed at
some microscopic crumbs on the table's oil-cloth, fussed at the frayed
edge for a moment until he recognized the gesture with horror as not
being his own (p. 12).

Sammler, of course, has had years to cope with his lonely grief,
whereas Berman is still struggling to understand a sudden,
heartrending loss. In doing so, he is inevitably reminded of the
earlier death of his son Marvin, and of his own proud, red-
bearded patriarch of a father, until he can scarcely rise beneath
the burgeoning weight of these accumulated griefs. At no time
are we distracted from viewing this inexorable working out of
the psychology of loss, although from the opening pages of the
novel Wallant manages to imply that something yet more
essential, more warping, underlies Berman's separation from life.
It would be too simple to view this as a simple loss of faith, a
failure to observe the old orthodoxies. Berman's dream-journies
into the past reveal not only a life ordered by ritual, but one
informed by a sensuous contact with nature which he has
progressively denied. It is thus no accident that he destroys the
plant which hangs in the kitchen, or that when, magicianlike, he
presses the silent switch in the bathroom, the flourescent lights
come out of the darkness "like artificial sunlight escaping a
cloud" (p. 13). The photograph of his son, which he can scarcely
bear to confront, shows the boy holding up the "ridiculously
small" fish he has caught. The rooms from which Berman feels so
estranged are papered in flower-covered patterns. The living
room threatens, too, with "the sealed-off fireplace with its neat
stack of white-birch logs" (p. 14) — so different from the real fire
which once warmed Berman in a Russian village. Scorning his
neighbor's ministrations to a frayed-looking cherry tree and a

lawn of "patchy, miserable grass," he thinks : "Give him a fifty by a hundred of good clean cement. These putterers, these after-hours artisans. If they had *worked* as *he* had worked in his life. . . ." (p. 12).

On the basis of such pointed imagery, it would be easy to picture Wallant as an enemy of modern times, the advocate of a nostalgic pastoralism; and, indeed, the recollections of a pastoral boyhood make this work almost unique within the urban tradition of the Jewish-American novel. But the dichotomy of modernism and pastoralism (or agrarianism) is not among the novel's articles of faith. Wallant clearly argues no return to a Jewish peasant society with its repressions, its *shtetl* mentality, the bloody rites of the pogrom; on the contrary, the author's romanticism frequently embraces the present (and the implied future), but never the past. What we are given in the richly articulated contrast between a cold, mechanical present and a warm, life-embracing past is the existential anguish that results when man abandons one set of values without finding a replacement sufficient to sustain him in moments of trial. Before he can live in the world again, Berman must find something to approximate the sense of communion with nature, of harmony with his fellow man, he had known as a child. If his painful odyssey into time past reminds him repeatedly of his losses, it also reminds him of his unused human capacities, and the joyous, healing relationship to the natural world becomes their measure.

III *The Lessons of the Past*

As the etchings of memory are unveiled, they repeatedly reveal a sense of communion with the natural world. Even in one of the earliest, dated September 1949, a recollection of the surprise party given for the Bermans' twenty-fifth anniversary, the natural world adds its affirmation to a feast of love and commitment—one strong enough, significantly, to distract Berman from the knowledge that his mother lies dying in hospital. As he and Mary approach the party, "the waves pounded on the beach far down the street and there was a smell of salt and rank mud and seaweed" (pp. 41-42). When he departs, laughing and singing with his family, their voices are "small in the depths of sea-damp air" (p. 44). Through it all, Berman senses that something has perhaps eluded him, winking brightly "at various moments like mysterious gems in a river bed: the Russian songs, the ocean sounds, the flash of his wife's proud blue dress" (p. 45). When his dream self retreats to the hot afternoon of July 22, 1934, he and his partner, Riebold, are driving toward the beach, where their families share a summer cottage. They arrive to an image of "bright yellow ears of corn . . . ranged on the table along with baskets of blackberries and crisp summer vegetables wet and still speckled with soil" (pp. 61-62). Berman plays with his children on the beach, wrestles with his partner, and makes unusually intense love to his wife: "The bed creaked in quiet spasms and the odor of love was mixed with that also spermy scent of cottages near the sea, salt-mixed, moldy, and rank" (p. 66). The moment is reminiscent of the Bermans' wedding day, and the seaside hotel to which they carry their awkwardly new, clumsy-fingered love.

But it is when Berman's mind spirals back to his Russian childhood that the sense of a healing, nurturing contact with nature is most dramatically sketched. He covets "the wild moments in the field or by the river" because they are circumscribed and hence made yet more precious by his father's stern edicts. When he plays with his youthful friends in a potato field, he senses that they are too old for such games, but only relishes them the more as "a symbol of things they yearned for with their inarticulate cries" (p. 131). The boys lie, exhausted by potato-throwing, wrestling, grappling, staring up at the Russian sky:

It was as though what they had thought to seize turned out only a breath, a scent, a thing as yet remote from them. The sky darkened, turned bluer, like water, showing greater and greater depths. The mocking call of a small bird came up from the tall grasses at the edge of the potato field and a lone crow carried the message in his coarser voice into the wood (p. 132).

It is then that the sallow, hysterical Rachel lures Berman away from his boyish games and encourages him to make love to her. Once more the natural images dominate:

They walked some distance, through a dense part of woods, then out to a little clearing where there were the remains of an ancient peasant hut. Butterflies flew over the humble ruins and there were fireflies on the ground darkness. The sky overhead was violet, and back to the east there were hazy summer stars in the part of the heavens already claimed by night (p. 135).

This first discovery of his own sensuality is dated July 1912. Dreams then carry Berman back to September 1910, when he faints from hunger on Yom Kippur, but refuses to break the fast. Rewarded for his faith by the "brief transfiguration" of a smile on his father's face, he waits outside the synagogue, "in the sighing breeze and sunlight, listening to the confined voices from inside the synagogue, trying to pick out the voices of his father and his brother. . . ." (p. 148).

As recollections of human communion and natural joy become more intense, more palpable in detail, Berman's life in the present becomes more mechanical and soporific. He plunges into the routine of his work, seeks the dulling narcotic of television, finds only temporary solace in boarders whose private wounds parody his own, toys with suicide, and becomes progressively dehumanized in his responses:

Going up his front steps he almost had the feeling of being physically engaged in some worn piece of machinery. There was a sense of automation, of knowing exactly what each movement would be, one after another, like a movie he had sat through innumerable times. There was no pleasure in it, only a sort of bleak ease, for it demanded nothing from him.

Push upward slightly as you turn the key. Door squeaks at the point of half-opening. Electric bill falls from the letter slot. And the *Jewish Ledger*. Walk through the living room and the dining room, careful to walk on the runner instead of the carpet. Through the kitchen where the stove rattles to your footfall, loud after the muffling carpets in the front rooms. Down the long hallway, past the bedrooms where nothing stirs, not even the curtains, for the windows are closed tight as though sealed (p. 128).

The sealed windows, like Berman's contempt for a neighbor's pathetic garden and his destruction of his wife's plant, signal his increasingly dangerous divorce from a world of natural rhythms and sounds. He finds the moon hazy and threatening, scorns the smell of cooking food in a black tenement house, and makes himself blind, behind streaked, dirty glasses, to the images of the world outside his private hell: "He waited on his front steps for Riebold, his eyes glazed against the passer-by, his ears deafened to the voices of children testing the day" (p. 48). Thus, he shuts the windows of the house "against the scent of the earth and the blossoms" (p. 51), and is angered by the calendar whose color photographs mock him with his own lost vision: "There was a spray-filled ocean beach, a blue-hazed mountain, and a broad river glinting in a summer sun . . ." (p. 51). The doom of his terrible loneliness is underscored when he awakens, stiffens himself for a new day, and dresses "with his eyes semiblind on the window, which opened on a brilliant summer day already redolent with sunwarmed smells of soil and flowers" (p. 106). Later, he brutishly breaks apart a plate with a sailboat on it that had been Mary's favorite, and on the following day grapples in a clownish parody of lust with the drunken cleaning-woman. Once more he renounces his daughter's plea that he help her mourn and turns his anger on her to declare, "See, I'm not crying for the good old days. I'm crying because I'm dead . . . worse than dead . . . in Hell. I feel only hate" (p. 144). Hoping that alcohol may dull his pain, he sits at the kitchen table and begins to drink in steady, silent desperation. Once more, the contrast of natural imagery and his own mechanical gestures is underscored: "Outside, the night was alive with little sounds: tinklings, chirpings, buzzings. Inside there was just the inhuman sound of his swallowing and the little bumps of the glass and the bottle as he moved them in undecipherable patterns" (p. 144).

IV   The New Discipline

Wallant does not demand that such images bear the urgent freight of symbolism, but their lyric repetition and clustering establish a crucial leitmotiv for the novel. As Berman's estrangement from nature becomes more acute, his gestures grow increasingly robotlike, until we see him in Chapter 13 as one point in the hollow triangle whose other points are marked by a whiskey bottle and a drinking glass. In this central chapter, in which he rejects his daughter, he has also scorned the clumsy but well-intentioned ministrations of his friend Riebold and startled a small boy with the grotesque mask his face has become. His ears sealed to the chorus of summer-night sounds that caress the house, he attempts suicide. Never was Wallant's language more precise, more heartrending in its very muted economies, than in his description of this ultimate act of the broken man's desperation:

"Oh, well," he said as he stood, offhand, as though at some tiny
consideration like the putting out of a light.

Slowly he walked down the hall to the bathroom. The light there was
a sudden violence and he squinted his eyes. He opened the medicine
cabinet, swinging the sight of his face away with the opening of that
mirrored door. There were two or three razor blades on the bottom
shelf. He studied them for a moment, then selected the one that had no
visible rust on it. He closed the cabinet door but kept his head down so
the face couldn't look at him.

Absently he ran the blade across the inside of his wrist in two
deliberate strokes. Then he put the blade down on the sink and
watched the two fine lines redden and thicken with blood, which hung
in the markings for a considerable time, held by the surface tension,
until finally, like a river overrunning its banks, it began to flood his wrist
with a dozen little meandering streams. He held his arm out from his
clothes as he moved over toward the toilet. Then he held it over the
bowl, watching how the thick drops fell into the water in the toilet and
spread there like veinous red blossoms.

Some of the blood began to run up his arms, so he tilted his hand
lower. His wrist was a wild crimson smear. Curiously he studied it, tried
to find importance in that innocuous, gaudy color.

Then he noticed the red splashings on the floor, one spot on the
immaculate gray throw rug. He made a little clucking sound behind his
teeth (pp. 144–45).

The pity and terror compressed into the single "clucking sound"
which terminates Berman's act of self-destruction are all the
more moving because of the near-mathematical detachment and
precision with which his actions are described.

When Wallant's technique faltered, or when he doubted the
emotive thrust of a phrase, his tendency was always to force his
meaning through metaphor and adverb—often with the most
clumsy effect. Here, however, other than the few adverbs which
denote simple physical conditions ("slowly," "down," "up,"
"lower"), there are only two which endow sentences with
dramatic moment, and both are strikingly unconventional.
Berman cuts lines across his wrists "absently"—a word that
suggests he is the living dead, that he has already become so
estranged from his own body it has ceased to have meaning for
him. And when he studies the gaudy color of his own blood, he
does so "curiously"—i.e., with curiosity, for the surge of blood,
the flow of life, is something whose meaning he has nearly
forgotten. The two metaphors in the passage are equally striking:

his blood flows from the cuts "like a river overrunning its banks," and drops into the toilet bowl to spread "like veinous red blossoms." Significantly, both metaphors of blood recall the excluded world of nature: the river that has been so central to Berman's vision of life, the flowers of his first love, of his marriage, of the very summer night from which he has shut himself away. Other details are equally poignant in suggestion. Ending his life means no more to Berman than "the putting out of a light." He avoids his face in the mirror, as he has on earlier occasions, because he is so totally estranged from the face of the stranger he would greet there. One is reminded, too, that the old Jewish custom of covering mirrors following a death has, like so many rituals, been ignored. Berman's habitual, almost compulsive sense of cleanliness and order—Jewish ritual transformed into bourgeois habit—instructs him to choose an unrusted blade, and the same trained, automatic response intercedes to save his life: the single drop of blood that falls onto "the immaculate gray throw rug."

The discipline of this crucial passage is the more remarkable as Wallant never, even in his late work, entirely controlled his penchant for melodrama. It is partly "his marvelous eye," to borrow a phrase which Dorothy Dudley applied to Theodore Dreiser, which saves him here. Dreiser, too, frequently lapsed into melodrama, or decked halting sentences in garlands of metaphor and adverb. One of the more notable examples of his lean, controlled style is, coincidentally, the description of Hurstwood's suicide near the conclusion of *Sister Carrie*. In this passage, the critical adjectives "leisurely," "softly," and "calmly" convey a moving charge of pathos:

Now he began leisurely to take off his clothes, but stopped first with his coat, and tucked it along the crack under the door. His vest he arranged in the same place. His old wet, cracked hat he laid softly upon the table. Then he pulled off his shoes and lay down.

It seemed as if he thought a while, for now he arose and turned the gas out, standing calmly in the blackness, hidden from view. After a few moments, in which he reviewed nothing, but merely hesitated, he turned the gas on again, but applied no match. Even then he stood there, hidden wholly in that kindness which is night, while the uprising fumes filled the room. When the odor reached his nostrils, he quit his attitude and fumbled for the bed.[1]

V   *The Horrid Anger of Bereavement*

Following his suicide attempt, Berman sinks deeper into Lethean numbness, his sole passion reduced to the flicker of insubstantial figures on the television screen. Meanwhile, he grows more and more blind to the real world. Turning to the entertainment page of the newspaper even before entering the house, he squints "at the small columns of tiny type, not just because the lenses of his glasses were dirty, but because he hadn't been to the eye doctor in two years and might never go now that there was no one to prod him" (p. 149). Cocooned by the clichés of a television serial, he scarcely registers his daughter's voice on the telephone, is deaf to her heartrending cry, "Daddy, Daddy, for God's sake have pity on me . . ." (p. 151). But despite the numbness in which he has armored himself, the revelations of his dream-life begin to intrude on these escapist hours. During the prizefights he seems to hear hoofbeats and the creaking of wheels, and he says aloud, "No, that trip to Kiev was another time" (p. 153). This first, brief intrusion, in Chapter 14, is the beginning of Berman's awakening to a new life. Though still "lost to his body and the horrid anger of his bereavement" (p. 159), he begins consciously to sift the encoded messages of the past. In Chapter 15, while washing himself after work, he remembers Kiev, the marketplace with its magical abundance, the taste of ice cream, the voice of his father. When the rabbi calls to offer Berman his practiced consolation, the old man's mind drifts again to the markets in Kiev, "and the smell of sheep and dust mingled with the scent of fallen leaves and trampled grapes and bruised, odorous apples" (p. 162). Seated in the wagon with his family, he looks dizzyingly up at "the great well of the heavens, the stars sprayed across it as from some gigantic explosion. . . . And larger still, seated beside the dim shape of his mother, the great figure of his father, swaying to the motion of the wagon so it seemed he prayed, so similar was his aspect to that of his swaying morning devotions" (p. 162).

On the night that follows, Berman dreams the most lyric and nurturing of his dreams. It is now an early morning in September 1907, and the wagon in which he travels with his mother, father, and brother draws near home. Surrendering to the comforting rhythm of the wagon, Yussel scarcely marks the boundary between sleeping and waking; colors and sounds flow about him

in a continuous litany, and he finds himself yearning for a sight of
the river:

Then it appeared, a broad, living reflection of the lightening sky,
merged with the shore on its edges where it mirrored distortedly the
pines and the spruces; and its sound up close was soft, yet so all-
embracing that it gave an impression of great volume, like a whisper
from a titan's throat (p. 164).

The river both entices him with its strength and beauty and
confirms that the family now draws near home, but not before
the message the river offers him has been summed up in a
startling epiphany:

A boat appeared on the broad current. A peasant and a boy were bent
over a net as their boat pulled against the anchoring rope. Suddenly
they pulled the net up into the boat, tumbling a confusion of silver. The
man looked toward the wagon rumbling along the deserted dawn road.
He called out something in a hoarse voice. Then he held a fish aloft in
his hand, a shape of brief sparkle and brilliance (p. 165).

And a single, brief nod from his father confirms to Yussel that he
has witnessed something wondrous.

This testament to the majesty and bounty of nature, to the
cycles of death and renewal—so reminiscent of the seaside
musings over the meaning of death in Whitman's "Out of the
Cradle Endlessly Rocking"—has been lost to Berman. The image
of the fish glinting in the sun recalls the photograph that hangs in
Berman's dead son's room—a picture of the gawky, half-grown
boy proudly holding up the small fish he has caught. Berman,
though once strengthened by his own stern father's wisdom and
devotion, had turned Marvin aside, never replying with the slow
nod of recognition and confirmation his questioning eyes had
once drawn from his own father. Significantly, it is during their
seaside holiday that Berman most pointedly refuses his son's plea
for recognition. Though he sees "a flicker of agony" in the boy's
eyes, he is unable to reach out to comfort him, and the boy
withdraws further into his lonely self.

VI   *The Demands of Filial Love*

The death of his wife, Mary, is the catalyst for Berman's grief,
but not its sole cause. In his lonely hours he is compelled, like
Bellow's dangling hero, Joseph, to contemplate the values and

the priorities of his life, and what is slowly, relentlessly revealed is a breach with life, with nature, with the Jewish codes of his boyhood, with family, and ultimately therefore with self. Central to this exploration of Berman's malaise is the relationship between fathers and sons that is a recurrent motif in American literature—from Redburn's confused attempts to comprehend the world with an outdated guidebook of his father's, through Huckleberry Finn's symbolic murder of his blood father and his ultimate, agonized acceptance of Nigger Jim, to Robert Jordan's obsession with his father's suicide in Hemingway's *For Whom the Bell Tolls* and Ike McCaslin's ritual initiation by Sam Fathers in Faulkner's *The Bear*. The Jewish-American writer has repeatedly and often agonizingly contemplated the theme—in part, perhaps, because the pressures of life in the New World so often eroded the authority and the majesty of the old patriarchs. Wallant's work thus suggests comparison with Henry Roth's *Call It Sleep,* Saul Bellow's "Father-to-Be," Bernard Malamud's "Idiots First" and *The Assistant,* Philip Roth's *Portnoy's Complaint,* Jonathan Baumbach's *A Man to Conjure With,* and Herbert Gold's *Fathers.*

Berman's indifference to demands of filial love is underscored by his lack of attention to the problems of the grandson who bears the dead Marvin's name, for in the Jewish faith this handing down of the name of a dead relative is a celebration of the renewal of life and a guarantee of the spiritual integrity of the dead. Furthermore, according to the *Code of Jewish Law,* the birth of a male child is itself redemptive of the family's grief: "If a male son is born in that family, the entire family is saved by it; but only a male, for when a male comes into this world, peace comes into the world."[2] Such intimations of immortality are lost on Berman, who prefers the masochistic indulgence of his own grief to the consolations of faith. Indeed, his excessive mourning of Mary is in open violation of a religion which forbids such excess:

Our Sages, of blessed memory, said again: "He who mourns for the dead to excess, will have cause to mourn for another death." This applies only to an ordinary person, but when a scholar passes away, his death is mourned in proportion to his wisdom. In no case, however, should the mourning period be more than thirty days, for none is greater than Moses our teacher, peace to him, of whom it is written (Deuteronomy 34:8): "And they wept for Moses thirty days."[3]

The respect for a higher power—perhaps even just for the power of creation, the renewing cycles of life—is implicit in such an injunction but for a time inaccessible to Berman, who has "come a long way from the old rituals," even though respect for God remains "buried in his forgetfulness."

VII   *Biblical Allusion*

Stripped of all allegiances which might help him contain his grief, Berman rages against his God and comes to see himself as Joblike in his sufferings, though it is in fact his well-intentioned but half-hearted rabbi who draws the literal comparison. Here, as in Wallant's later works, biblical allusions help to structure the mosaic pattern of the prose. Eclectically he interweaves Jewish and Christian experience, not in order to create modern-day parables or translations of ancient experience, but to add resonance and dimension to the story of the insignificant men—a plumber, a pawnbroker, a hospital orderly, and a rent-collector—who serve as his heroes. Joblike, Berman addresses his curses to an unintelligible god who seems to make sport with his life, and then to ignore his "doom of loneliness." His partner, his daughter, his rabbi all offer up the meaningless and worn consolations offered by Job's counselors. And as Job sits in the dung-heap in his deepest abnegation, so Berman descends into a filthy cellar which seems the corollary to his spiritual despair:

The cellar was ancient. Filth covered every stanchion and wall like thick paint. Small puddles of stagnant water shone with dull darkness in the feeble light from the high, dirty windows. Every time he moved, Berman felt the little wisps of spider web brush his face and the smell of urine and feces was very strong around where he was working. But his revulsion was so old and habitual that he was hardly conscious of it, and worked expressionlessly to the sound of footsteps on the floor over his head (pp. 24-25).

Ultimately, God speaks to the despairing Job, his voice emanating from the whirlwind to sing of the goodly wings of peacocks, the nostrils of grasshoppers, and other signs of God's terrible power. "Canst thou draw out leviathan with a hook?" he questions Job (Job, 41:1). No, a chastened Berman might answer, only a single, small fish, to gleam golden in the sun.

It is not, however, the almighty creator whose Old Testament voice reprimands and consoles the latter-day Job, but the small, tyrannous domestic godhead that television has become for him. In Chapter 16, dated August 1956, Berman gives himself up to an "evening of television and strange musings" (p. 169). He has forgotten even the comforting, automatic gestures which made him a good workman, once more brushed away Riebold's clumsy ministrations, hung up the telephone on his anxious daughter. As he watches the miniature drama on the television screen, his mind drifts back to the pines that were "a blue-green screen for the black river" (p. 169), recalls his joy in the scent of the "bitter river mud, the Russian earth, wild flowers blended in like part of the recipe with the frail smell of his mother's bread" (p. 169). Often, he would plunge knee-deep into the velvet mud at the river's edge, daring his father's wrath, and at night "from the depths of his feather bed, . . . he heard the river singing," mixed with "his father's deep, bearded voice and the high-soft plea of his mother's comfort . . ." (p. 170). What Wallant offers here is both more and less than a return to the old orthodoxy. A boy standing beside a swiftly flowing river, a family gathered by the warmth of the hearth, the lighting of sabbath candles, voices raised in prayer: all constitute a plea for a renewed sense of harmony, of rhythm and essential respect for life. And twining through such images of comfort and nurture is the bland mechanical voice of the television huckster, touting "this cleaner in a bottle, this miracle cleaner that cleans your walls, your car, your dog; maybe your soul, too?" (p. 170). A news program shows a rocket arching into space—yet more worship of a technology which does nothing for the anguished, dislocated soul of man. Suddenly the screen goes black, and like a junkie deprived of his fix, Berman loses control, ripping off the back of the television set and groping through the bewildering maze of tubes and wiring. "A panic came over him at the lifelessness of the mechanism. Just by his wild groping he hoped to breathe life into it" (p. 171). But life will not emanate from Berman until he can reach out to his fellow man, and the machine answers his gropings only with a massive electrical shock, a travesty of the life force he has sought: "Suddenly ferocious life snaked up his arm and reached for his heart. He gave a loud cry as the electricity shot through him. He felt himself thrown, as though by a gigantic hand, down to the floor. Stunned he lay there" (p. 171). And this massive shock rends his spirit as it rends his flesh, so that Berman begins to weep and then to pray: "Baruch atah Adoni . . . God in Heaven . . . Mary, Mary, my

wife . . . forgive me . . . V'yiskadash . . . Gott in Him-
mel . . . forgive me . . ." (p. 171). This is the blow that breaks
the spirit's sleep, and it will have its corollary in the novels which
succeed this one. In his macaronic prayer, a jumble of English,
Russian, and Yiddish, Berman discovers the message of these
suffering months:

For the first time in his life he knew, as he hadn't known even in his
deepest despair and rage, that there was no Enemy, no Betrayer, no
bearded Torturer; and for a minute or two that knowledge froze him in
a fearful grief that made all the other suffering like a child's
peevishness beside it. He was alone (p. 172).

VIII   A Craving for Humanity

No beneficent God restores to Berman his fields and flocks, his
family and chattels; but he is restored to life, and out of his own
tormented spirit he will spin the web of a new, authentic self.
Suddenly, a craving comes over him—not for physical nourishment, but for "the street, the people who strolled by, the ground,
the stars" (p. 172), and as he drifts to sleep later, he seems to
hear "the river, singing that one glorious monotony" (p. 172).
The past, dredged up in his dream life, provides him now with
the energy and zeal for commitment, community and love in the
present. As Joyce Rudell has observed, "Wallant appears to
borrow from Wordsworth the idea that the child is father of the
man, and that in a divine state of innocence also resides the
special capacity to feel and experience natural correspondences,
transcendent emotions and poetic glimpses of immortality.
Embroidering the mystical condition of childhood, Wallant
suggests Berman's own beginning as the mythical starting point
for birth and constant renewal."[4]

Water—the ancient symbol of life—plays a central role in
establishing this mythical dimension to the novel. Not only are
Berman's most transcendent memories associated with the river,
with seaside adventures and demonstrations of strength, with the
fisherman who (both Christ and Fisher King) so proudly shares
his gleaming trophy; Berman himself is a plumber; he takes pride
in cleansing himself to be worthy of Mary, and when his despair
takes away his workman-like skills, causes him to bungle jobs,
Riebold protests, "The water is shut off, the people are without
water" (p. 166).

Following the revelation that no malicious deity is to blame for his griefs, Berman throws open the windows of the house, and with a "curious sense of quest" sets out for a day at the beach. He thinks of his journey as a "pilgrimage," and with mild amusement recalls "the religious men in Russia who traveled great distances to visit some miracle rabbi" (p. 175). His earthy, ribald comrade, Riebold, had once thought of Berman as just such a miracle rabbi, and he is now prepared to fulfill that calling. He rejoices in the sights and sounds of the streets, in the bus ride that takes him to the ocean, in the antics of the bathers, and even in the fierce, uncompromising heat of the sun. But all day storm clouds gather on the horizon, and Berman fears that perhaps some malevolent force does look down at him from the heavens. He returns to New Haven and walks through a section of town populated by Italians and blacks still struggling to achieve the American Dream whose minor badges Berman has earned the right to wear. There he stops to watch a fist-fight outside a tavern, and a policeman demands that he be a witness. Instinctively, Berman recoils from this commitment: " 'A witness?' " Berman said. " 'No, no, I'm not from around here, count me out.' " And the policeman responds that he must "testify": "That you was here, that you saw everything. Like it or not, you *were* here. You saw it all . . ." (pp. 183–184). And, indeed, Berman has seen "all," has borne witness, and must now accept the consequences of his vision. Berman gives the policeman his name, and his mind fills with the shifting, changing images of the crowded humanity that surrounds him. Suddenly the rain begins to fall, and like a child Berman walks home in the torrent, "smelling through cleared nostrils the rain-softened ground and the crushed flowers" (p. 187). His rebirth is complete; only the ceremonial baptism remains:

He took off his glasses and carried them in his hand, for they were useless in the flooding rain. It gave his face a peculiar, naked look, a blind almost terrible expression of trustfulness. . . . He appeared awful and strange, walking so slowly, blindly, submissive and aimless in the down-pour (p. 187).

Seen in context of the Jewish faith, this washing corresponds to the bath which the mourner takes on the thirtieth and last day of his observance of grief; it signals his return to the world. For Berman there are no more dreams, and in the final chapter of the novel he sits in the empty house, waiting for his son-in-law to call for him and take him home. If the hero's moment of triumphant self-recognition lacks the tragic resonance of *The Pawnbroker* and *The Children at the Gate* or the comic bravura of *The Tenants of Moonbloom*, it nonetheless moves the reader with its quiet dignity, its philosophical integrity, the richly articulated poetry of the commonplace.

IX   *Jewish Law and Christian Dimension*

As in Wallant's next published novel, *The Pawnbroker*, and in *Gimple the Fool*, which he began shortly after completing *The Human Season*, Jewish history and custom play major roles in the novel. Often, indeed, an individual gesture can be adequately translated only by reference to Jewish law. When Berman rejects his daughter's anguished plea that she help him mourn, he denies not only a human obligation but a religious law. Berman's own dying father had begged for the Kaddish, and the Jewish prayers for the dead do not mourn the passing of life; indeed, death itself is not even mentioned in the prayer. Instead, it celebrates the continuity of life and the community of the living. "He will swallow up death forever; and the Lord God will wipe away tears from all faces," the mourners chant from the book of *Isaiah* (25:8), and death cedes its dominion. This Jewish attitude toward mourning is vital to the conclusion of *The Pawnbroker*, as it is to an appreciation of the concluding prayer for the dead in Saul Bellow's *Mr. Sammler's Planet.* A situation in Bernard Malamud's intricate, moving short story "The Mourners," which is reminiscent of an episode in *The Tenants of Moonbloom*, graphically illustrates this attitude. Malamud records a landlord's efforts to evict an ancient tenant whose apartment fills with rotting garbage. When even legal maneuvers fail, the landlord, Gruber, goes to the old man to reason with him, only to find him "bunched up there on the floor engaged in an act of mourning." Stunned, frightened, the landlord finally concludes, "Somebody's dead. . . . He figured Kessler had got bad news, yet instinctively knew he hadn't. Then it struck him with a terrible force that the mourner was mourning him: it was *he* who was dead." And as the landlord stares in amazement at the room, he sees it suddenly as "clean, drenched in daylight and fragrance."[5] Suffering unbearable remorse for his treatment of the old man, the landlord sinks to the floor in an act of compassion and contrition, to join in the communal act of mourning. And having no prayer shawl, he tears the sheet from Kessler's bed, wraps it round his shoulders, and begins to pray. For Malamud as for Wallant and Bellow, this ritual of prayer is an affirmation of the brotherhood of man.

Not only must certain gestures and allusions in the novel be seen in context of Wallant's own Jewish background; some of the novel's most memorable scenes dramatize Jewish family life in the *shtetl*. The episode recalled from April 1909, when Joseph proudly walks beside his father into the unsuspected anti-Semitic trap laid for them in the allegorical Street of the Butchers, is the most chilling of these, but even here the father proves himself as Moseslike redeemer, who strikes out at the face of bigotry and hatred. Thus, this terrifying moment becomes for the boy "a time of surging glory," so unlike what he can share with his own son. Indeed, when the news of Marvin's death is brought to Berman, he is at work in a munitions factory, playing his own role in the complex machinery of death and destruction; and his blind dedication to technology, to the mechanical, disembodied, flowerless god of the machine will finally make him the temporary acolyte of the television set.

Yet despite the pervasive context of Judaism in which the story unfolds, Wallant also endows it with Christian dimension. Joseph's dead wife was named Mary; his rebirth is confirmed by Christian (and pagan) baptism. Wallant's vision of life is profoundly religious, but never narrowly doctrinaire. In his later writings allusions to Judaism will be few, but his faith in man's ability to renew his spirit will be strengthened. Even in this early work there is ample evidence of that generosity of vision which informed both Wallant's life and his work; and though *The Human Season* must in many respects be ranked as an apprentice novel, it contains abundant evidence of the author's extraordinary talent. His ability to create meticulously defined minor characters often shows a Dickensian vitality of inventiveness. Berman's two boarders, for example, each of whom represents an aspect of himself he either despises or fears, are portrayed with painful exactitude. When Berman rejects the first of them, the compulsive masturbator who occupies the room of Berman's rejected son, Wallant's novelistic skill is triumphant:

"Well, you can thh-hhh-hh-think what you w-want, Mr. Berman, but I certainly w-w-will not burden you w-w-huh my huh. . . ." His

stretched-open mouth revealed the remains of the meat sandwich
around his tiny, immature teeth. Suddenly his eyes stretched open so
wide it seemed the membrane split and they overflowed (p. 95).

The narrative genius sometimes flowers in a single phrase, as
when Berman recalls a black woman's hearty laughter so vividly
that it rings "faintly in the van behind him as though someone
had tapped sharply on one of the lengths of pipe" (p. 49). Yet the
novel is not entirely free of the clumsiness of the other early
works (as when he describes the windows of Berman's house as
being "like the empty sockets in a dead face" (p. 69) or from the
deadliness of cliché: "The lights of other houses twinkled
through the trees all around him, teasing him like so many bright
eyes, with mystery and promise and the goodness of life" (pp.
104-5).

But such lapses are happily rare exceptions. In *The Human
Season* Wallant gives us, on the primary level, a painfully
believable case study of grief, and on the book's intricate
metaphorical level, a moving account of man's innate capacity
for regeneration. Wallant had entitled an earlier version of the
novel *A Scattering on the Dark,* and for a time considered calling
it, simply, *Berman.* The former title was borrowed from
Archibald MacLeish's poem "Einstein," in which the scientist
meditates on the contrast between his own finite nature and the
seeming infinity of the universe. The poem culminates in a vision
of Einstein's death:

> Like a foam
> His flesh is withered and his shriveling
> And ashy bones are scattered on the dark.
> But still the dark denies him. Still withstands
> The dust his penetration and flings back
> Himself to answer him.
> Which seems to keep
> Something inviolate. A living something.[6]

The Human Season is Wallant's moving tribute to that
"Something inviolate" in man which cannot be dispersed even in
the last withering of flesh, the scattering of ashes on the dark.

CHAPTER 4

"Gimple the Beast"

I *Comic Vocalizing*

LONELINESS and deprivation are painfully etched into both *The Human Season* and *The Pawnbroker*, but Wallant's generous gifts as a comic writer are also abundantly apparent in those novels. The vision of all his work is essentially comic in its joyful, Chassidic sense of the ultimate triumph over adversity, and in the ritual pattern of his heroes' experiences, so similar to Northrop Frye's sense of the comic sequel to tragedy:

If we are right in our suggestion that romance, tragedy, irony and comedy are all episodes in a total quest-myth, we can see how it is that comedy can contain a potential tragedy within itself. In Myth, the hero is a god, and hence he does not die, but dies and rises again. The ritual pattern behind the catharsis of comedy is the resurrection that follows death, the epiphany or manifestation of the risen hero. . . .[1]

Wallant's work is rich in precisely such epiphanies, although in his earlier writings the novelist's tone is more somber than in the late works. His virtuoso comic voice was first fully articulated in *The Tenants of Moonbloom,* but his comic vocalizing had in fact begun in a manuscript which he started immediately after completing *The Human Season,* abandoned in order to write *The Pawnbroker,* and then returned to briefly, though without producing a finished manuscript. Not merely because it foreshadows the generous humor of the later works, but also for the light it throws on Wallant's attitudes at the time he wrote *The Pawnbroker,* the unfinished novel *Gimple the Beast* merits detailed consideration.

In the earliest version of the novel, tentatively entitled *Harold and Gimple,* Wallant sketches the collapse of a middle-class

61

Jewish marriage. Abe Gimple, the husband, is a kosher butcher, a man of fierce energies and lusts whose intense love affair with life is threatening both to his children and to his quiet, rather prim wife, Ada. The earliest account of Gimple's misadventures is seen largely through the eyes of his adopted son Harold, an office worker who keeps books for his father, frets about being drafted, and agonizes about his own paternity. Gimple's own sons, Paul and Martin, are soldiers, but Harold presumes that a history of scarlet fever will keep him out of the army, although the tensions of his waiting game with the draft board progressively aggravate his insecurities about his own manhood. Gimple, meanwhile, begins to rail against progressive intimations of mortality. He smashes a delicate porcelain teacup that he associates with his wife's feminine placidity, and strikes her breast. Ultimately , he collides with Harold, who denounces him as "a big clown." "Your painting, your singing—they're just big jokes," Harold says. Later, Harold witnesses Gimple's minor heart attack when he overstrains himself lifting barbells, and almost imperceptibly, Harold realizes that, whatever his own biological paternity, the fiercely energetic man is his true father.

II   The Butcher Clown

This early version of the Gimple novel is diluted by the story of Harold, and the dramatic focus of Wallant's work seems badly askew. In his notes, the figure of Gimple grows stronger and stronger, more compelling, and more dense in texture, until the butcher-fool dominates Wallant's conception as he dominates his wife and children. But meanwhile, Harold yearns to be something more than "a barely distracting corner vision image in everyone's eyes," tries to see himself as "the tragic clown," concocts ornate schemes—the assassination of the president, bombing the Empire State Building, raping a great woman—to draw attention to himself, but in the end is reduced to the commonplaces of the near-at-hand. As Harold's warped love for Gimple baffles and enrages him, Wallant compares the tormented boy to Raskolnikov, and prepares for the novel's tragic conclusion.

Seeking release from a baffling conflux of emotions, Harold stabs Gimple, only to yearn desperately to be in the dead man's place, to save him; unable to do so, he kills himself. In an early chapter outline of the novel, Gimple is killed by his adopted son Marvin, who then commits suicide. Wallant notes, "They looked like lovers." It is not merely the embarrassing melodrama of the ending which spoils *Harold and Gimple*, or even the schizophrenia of the novel's point of view, but the author's failure to realize the full dimensions of a superbly original comic portrait. In *The Pawnbroker* Wallant would explore further, and with far greater dramatic and philosophical moment, the relationship of teacher and apprentice, father and son, and the death of Jesus Ortiz will owe much to the terrifying moment when Harold yearns to take the dead butcher's place. But the stories of Harold and Gimple begin to diverge in Wallant's manuscript, and clearly the latter is too large, too vital and compelling, to occupy any position save that at center stage. In a holograph page which he wrote shortly after completing this first, unsatisfying version of the novel, Wallant gave his butcher hero a monologue which points toward the richer comic conception to be explored in *Gimple the Beast:*

God, I seen him a hundred thousand times. Here he is—in the flesh. See these eyes—this mouth, them ears, feel this heart—There's your God. And inside my head and between my legs and in my muscles. All them things. I can see the stars, I can feel the snow, I can taste and hear, I can screw and yell and dream and things is beautiful to me, beautiful!"

"Oh, no, you're no good alone—You need all the others, the murderers, the idiots, the crooks—all of them. It makes different colors, different sounds. What kind of band has only xylophones? No, you need the whole mess."

"What do I hate? Oh I'm not saying they shouldn't be—Otherwise I wouldn't have the fun of tryin' to destroy them. But I hate the phonies, the hypocrites who kill with money and lies. I hate certain kinds of liars."

"God, death? I'm not no philosopher—not much. I only know about life. And when I go I would like to drag everything with me—to leave just a big empty hole in the universe. Because when I go, Goddam it to hell everything goes!"

Gimple's Whitmanesque celebration of mankind and manunkind, in all its perplexing diversity, is lyric prelude to the visions of life with which all Wallant's later heroes will be possessed after their awakenings.

III   *The Obscenity of Death*

In the further, incomplete drafts of *Gimple the Beast,* the critical relationship of father and son is retained, though the figure of Harold disappears from Wallant's conception. Gimple, however, remains the vigorously life-asserting kosher butcher who paints wildly abstract canvases, writes romantic poetry, continually builds furniture that is never completed, adores his customers, reads voraciously, and lifts barbells. The broken teacup, the blow to Ada's breast, the collapse while lifting barbells are all retained. Ada and her raucous husband have three children—a thirty-three-year-old adopted son named Jerry, a divorced daughter, Sylvia, who writes children's books, and a schoolteacher son named Martin. Like Harold, Jerry occupies a central role in the novel, though his point of view remains subordinate to Gimple's. When he first began to rework the novel, Wallant gave each of the characters a section of his own, but alternate drafts suggest he abandoned the idea, for in comparison to "the great prowling shape of the mad butcher" his children seemed painfully anemic.

Angered at the encroachments of old age, Abe Gimple becomes even more raucous and foul-mouthed than before, and when he has a mild heart seizure while lifting barbells in the back of the butcher shop, intensifies yet more his bearish embrace of life; at this moment Wallant for the first time reveals the splendid range of his comic voice:

Gimple started for the front of the shop and Mendel warned him, "Put your shirt on, it's a lady."

But the butcher came out the way he was, his chest hair matted with sweat, his great arms gleaming. His face was dangerous and wild as with a strange defiance as he came behind the counter and looked at the woman.

"I saw your light . . . I didn't think you would be open. . . ." She stared nervously at the half-naked giant behind the counter, glanced at the door, then set her lips and studied the case which had been emptied of meat. "I don't suppose you would have an end-of-steak," she said doubtfully, hoping he wouldn't so she could get out of there.

"Sweet lady, I got all kinds of good flesh. I got beef of all sorts, lambs and calves. Every organ I got in *abundance,*" he said, widening his eyes suggestively. "Look, look at me, don't I look like a man well supplied with what a lady needs?"

Her face whitened, went from apprehension to anger.

"Don't tease yourself with doubt, darling. Come, come behind the counter and let Gimple show you his wares."

"You've seen the last of me, Mr. Gimple. Someone will hear about your behavior," she said grimly as she went to the door.

"What, are you offended, sweetie? I'm just a lusty butcher."

"I'll tell you what you are," she said from the doorway, one foot outside. "You are a dirty old man!" She slammed the door and was gone.

For a few minutes Gimple stood without moving, his smile pasted on his mouth and forgotten there. Mendel breathed softly in his terror. He watched the hairy skin twitch as with a sudden chill, or like a horse with an unreachable flea on it.

After a very long time, when the windows were completely black and the street was still outside, he turned to the old man, his smile queer and twisted on his meaty lips.

"ME OLD?"

It echoed in that place which had never been capable of echoes before, left a moaning sound in Mendel's ears like a great howl of wind. "OHHHH-HHLDD. . . ."

Suddenly he laughed. Then he began singing so savagely some old Russian song that Mendel moaned and covered his eyes.

But while Gimple sang with his great, laughing mouth, his eyes were furious and haunted.

As Gimple assures his adopted son, he is not so much afraid of getting old as angered by the violations his body now renders the spirit, and hence he is at first pleased to learn that a young Polish girl to whom he once recommended *Madame Bovary* is pregnant with his child. When Martin, Gimple's schoolteacher son, learns the news in a bar where the girl's Polish father talks about getting money from the "Jew butcher," he starts a fight with the construction worker and is badly beaten. When Ada learns the news, she demands a divorce. She asks Jerry to begin the proceedings, and when he tries to explain her feelings to his foster father, Gimple replies, "But she has laughed and been wild with me." Jerry's continued efforts to convince Gimple of the moralities involved provoke the following testament to life— one which Joe Berman and Sol Nazerman begin to grasp only after the awakenings that conclude their estrangement from life:

"Hey, let me tell you something, *boychick*. There's nothing bad except being dead—above ground or under. There's nothing wrong except to be cautious and stingy with yourself. Don't listen to all them in churches and synagogues, don't pay attention to teachers and moralists. There's no laws they can think of to cover you. You're one person, all alone and different, completely new. How could they have laws for people when each one is something that never was before. . . . You got a body, you got a brain, you might even have a soul. Use it all—there's no saving for another life. I mean this is all there is . . ." He looked around wonderingly as though he had suddenly found himself in another place. "And, my god . . . it's a lot, *boychick*, it's an awful lot."

No doubt Wallant could not entirely have endorsed a hedonism which estranges his character from community, yet the very language he gives to the bullying butcher underscores the novelist's enthusiasm for this heady assertion of life. "Anyhow," as Gimple later qualifies, "it's no easy thing to be a man, a *man*."

To meet the expenses of his new bachelor existence, Gimple gets a job two nights a week as a barker in an amusement park. He hires a lawyer and a private detective to seek evidence against Ada with which he could fight the divorce, and he is saved from a fierce beating by the Polish father and his thuggish comrades only through Martin's intervention. Confronted by Ada's lawyer, Gimple contends that his family all love him, and the lawyer's accusation that he knows nothing about love provokes another of Gimple's monologues, one which might serve as a coda to all of Wallant's writings:

"Love—it's a funny one all right. To tell the truth, I get it all mixed up myself," Gimple said. "It's something you feel . . . what, a sort of throb, excitement. No, not always that either, sometimes a sad, sad feeling—you would like to cry. Or laugh or yell or piss on the snow. I don't know. Sometimes I love the meat I chop; sometimes I love the drunk *schwartzas;* sometimes I love women's bodies; sometimes my children. What, it's perverted or something? Who cares! On the other hand, I get a holy, serious feeling looking at Ada's naked body. Sometimes she makes me feel like crying. Other times I'd like to get on top of her and screw around the clock. I love the sound of the air and I love the look of a dog's yellow turd lying in the Sunday morning sun. I love the smell of meat, raw and bloody. I love myself and sometimes I love my enemies. Maybe, right now I even love you, little fella. You see, that's love—Go try and figure!"

At this point, the manuscript breaks off with a handwritten note: "Jerry's and Ada's foremost." No doubt, it was the wife's and adopted son's points of view which Wallant intended to stress in the conclusion of the novel. Jerry, like the earlier Harold, would ultimately recognize his real father in Gimple, and Ada would contemplate the irreparable loss of this primal source of energy in her life. Jerry's concluding section seems never to have been written, but Ada's would no doubt have closely resembled the situation sketched in Wallant's short story "Death of an Enemy." In a final chapter outline for the novel, in which Jerry has become a young lawyer whose parents died many years before and who has always been drawn to "the wild and unpredictable Abe Gimple," the following conclusion is outlined:

Chapter 31
Ada comes home with Jerry late one afternoon. He is to have dinner there as he does at least three nights a week. There is the sound of someone in the pantry—a crash. They run in. Ada stands just in the doorway so Jerry can see her face and beyond her to where Gimple is falling, pulling the shelves and dishes, striking his head, to finally end up, half sitting up on the floor, his head resting against the wall. There are some words between Ada and Gimple and many silences whose meanings Jerry can only guess at. A long time seems to pass. There is the distant sound of the parade on Whalley Avenue drawing itself out fainter and fainter. And Gimple dies . . . defeating them.

Chapter 32
The funeral in the cemetery and later at home. Ada rubs her shoulder from time to time. The wind seems to bear a sound of laughter at the cemetery. At home they surround themselves with the food and the commiserations. Ada tells them, "It's a relief—in spite of everything. I can be sure of peace and have no more of pain from him." Continues to rub shoulder which hurts very little now.
But then, late at night after everyone but Jerry and the children are gone, in the great hollow emptiness of the hour, Ada says suddenly in a stunned, bewildered voice, "All of a sudden the pain in my shoulder is gone. And you know . . . it's very strange. For some reason I just feel all dead and buried myself."
Sylvia begins to cry terribly and Paul sits with his hands over his face shuddering. Martin rubs his forehead against the window looking fantastically furious as he looks at the interminable night. But Ada just sits there touching her shoulder, bewildered at the sudden loss of pain. Then she sighs and lowers her hand to her lap. She looks quite peaceful and her face is expressionless as she repeats almost absently, as though someone might not have heard her the first time, "All dead and buried myself."

IV   The Limitations of Monologue

In a sense, *Gimple the Beast* inverts the ritual pattern of Wallant's four published novels, in which characters progress from anomie to commitment, from death-in-life to the celebration that attends discovery of the authentic self. As the tentative outline of the final chapters of *Gimple* suggests, Ada herself has now lapsed into that numbed anonymity out of which Wallant's other characters struggle to be born. Furthermore, in Gimple's irreverent, inventively comic monologues, the author's own passionately affirmative vision of life is vigorously articulated. Yet in each of the numerous outlines for the novel, and in the several manuscript versions which exist, this majestically comic hero dies, and even though his very death suggests a transcendence of life ("The wind seems to bear a sound of laughter at the cemetery."), Wallant seems unable to cope with this inversion of his own mythology. Greater maturity would permit him to be comic without sacrificing seriousness of purpose, and more subtle command of the writer's craft would help him avoid the clumsiness, the narrative obscurities, of this early study of the clown. The Gimple manuscripts are setting-up exercises which prepare Wallant for the portraits of Sammy Cahan and Norman Moonbloom, and for what promised to be his funniest, most serious, most tender portrait of the fool, the estranged father of *Tannenbaum's Journey*. Gimple is perhaps viewed too exclusively from the outside—by his children, his wife, his friend Mendel—so that his moments of self-revelation are restricted to the monologues. Otherwise, we know him only through his outrageous conduct, the joyous idiosyncrasies which bear close enough resemblances to those of Saul Bellow's *Henderson the Rain King* to suggest that the Gimple novels, begun sometime in 1960, were inspired by Bellow's 1959 publication. Bellow, too, has difficulty in penetrating the inner consciousness of his hero and tends to rely on mannerism, stylistic bravura, and the contrived monologues of Henderson's tutorials in the lion's den with King Dahfu.

Wallant abandoned the Gimple novel with tremendous reluctance, and the figure of the passionate pilgrim he had created there was to become permanently resident in his novelistic imagination. When, in October 1961, he began the first and only notebook he ever kept, he sketched the outlines for a new novel to do with a rent-collector named Norman, and in these early musings about the narrative situation that was to become *The Tenants of Moonbloom*, Norman is Gimple's son. "To Norman," Wallant writes, "he was almost a hallucination, a huge, wild figure that banged into his life from time to time and then was gone again." A later note compares him to "a God who reaches down occasionally—on his Olympus of heedless pantheistic joy—full of life himself but not yet part of it in the way Norman is. That Norman is able to drink it all in should increase him to an even greater stature than the legendary Gimple." In these brief notes, Wallant reveals a further reason, and perhaps the most essential, for his inability to complete Gimple's story. In a single character, he had struggled to encompass his own vision of the comedy of affirmation, to create a titanic version of the father sought by all his fictional lost sons, and a fictional substitute, as well, for his own invalid father. But Wallant lacked the skill to produce a novelistic structure large enough to house such a giant, and perhaps lacked the confidence in his own redemptive vision to accept the death of his hero. Furthermore, before he could explore the full range of the comic point of view, he had to examine—more stringently and urgently than in *The Human Season*—the depths of negation and despair which are the landscape of *The Pawnbroker*.

CHAPTER 5

The Pawnbroker

I *The Literature of Holocaust*

A S numerous critics have observed, the American Civil War
produced thousands of books by men and women who had
witnessed some aspect of the conflict at first hand, but scarcely a
single work which possessed genuine literary distinction. In
1877, Horace Scudder, editor of the *Atlantic Monthly*, specu-
lated on this failure of imaginative vitality:

> We stand, perhaps, too near the scenes of the late war, and are too
> much a part of the conflict, to be able to bear the spectacle of that
> drama reenacted on the stage; but in due time the events not so much
> of the war as of the moral and political conflicts will find adequate
> presentation, when the best proportions of the theme will be reduced
> in epitome and made vivid in action, which concentrates the thought of
> the historic movement into a few characters and situations.[1]

Scudder's specific allusion is to drama, but his remarks might
easily be extended to encompass fiction, for the most vital and
accomplished novel of the Civil War, *The Red Badge of Courage*,
was to be written by a young man who had never even seen a
battlefield. Furthermore, Scudder's suggestion that audiences
stood too near the real events of the war has equal relevance to
the writers themselves, who required more historical perspective, more detachment, in order to assess the true moral and
political implications of the civil conflict and distill them into
representative actions and scenes. Such detachment becomes all
the more essential when the actual events of the war, and their
ethical implications, are so vast, so debilitating, so complex and
horrific as those of the American Civil War or of the Second
World War.

It is scarcely surprising that in the two decades following the surrender of Germany and Japan in 1945, most of the fiction dealing with World War II was naturalistic or documentary in style. Even the best of these novels, Norman Mailer's *The Naked and the Dead*, does little to assess the moral and philosophical implications of the new technological warfare, and it seems improbable that any novel could aesthetically encompass the obscene horrors of the Nazi holocaust. It would be unfair to expect the novelist to speculate about the causes of the war, but hardly inappropriate to expect him to reflect on its meaning, although time was clearly necessary to create the perspectives that would make possible such imaginative speculations and reconstructions. The Beat Generation and their contemporaries agonize in the 1950s over the implications of America's decision to drop the atomic bomb, but it is not until the beginning of the next decade that the novel effectively explores World War II in the manner that Scudder suggests when he urges that "the best proportions of the theme be reduced in epitome and made vivid in action." Joseph Heller's *Catch-22* and Edward Lewis Wallant's *The Pawnbroker* both appeared in 1961, and both novels offer shockingly graphic portrayals of the horrors of the war. Furthermore, despite their striking differences in tone, point of view and milieu, these works similarly urge that the human spirit is too resilient, the will to life too compelling, for individual man to surrender either to absurdity or to despair.

II   *A Truce of Survival*

The hero of Wallant's second published novel is a Polish Jew who survived the atrocities of a Nazi concentration camp with his life if not his spirit intact. The mutilations he endured, the destruction of his family, and his painfully vivid nightmares make him seem far older than his forty-five years. A former professor at the University of Cracow, Sol Nazerman goes to Paris after the war and then to the United States, to take a job as assistant to a New York pawnbroker. Eventually the refugee is offered his own shop, to be used as a channel for unreportable income by a petty racketeer. Thus, Nazerman himself becomes a pawn, a link in the chain of human exploitation and corruption of which the fragmented, dream-ridden world of the pawnshop is a microcosm. But the money he earns allows Nazerman to keep his privacy inviolate, to support his sister and her family, and to contribute to the needs of his part-time mistress, Tessie Rubin, who keeps continual deathwatch over her mutilated father. Only seven scenes in the novel deal with the Nazi death camps, though their grim legacy permeates the structure of the novel, as indelibly etched there as the blue numbers on the arms of Sol, Tessie and her father, and the professional refugee, Goberman. Nazerman's nightmares, in which he recalls horrifically, obscenely detailed incidents from the war, are unforgettable reminders of the holocaust, but Wallant's genius is to see them— without obscuring their particularity or their historical rele-vance—as distilled examples of the human legacy of cruelty and oppression. The grotesques who haunt Nazerman's Harlem pawnshop offer parallels in almost endless permutation to the torture and loss he endured. It is the pawnbroker's tragedy that he cannot recognize this community of grief—a tragedy he compounds, in his blindness, by joining the ranks of the exploiters.

Nazerman's delicate truce of survival will be rudely violated as the fifteenth anniversary of his family's death approaches and the pawnbroker is compelled to assume the "great aggregate of pains" his customers bring him. His awakening to the torturous responsibilities of feeling is largely provoked by his young black assistant, Jesus Ortiz, who lusts for the wealth and power of his master's knowledge. The relationship of Catholic apprentice and Jewish master may well have been suggested to Wallant by Bernard Malamud's *The Assistant*, published in 1957. Here, as in Wallant's novel, love is the redemptive grace that transforms a tortured world. Frank Alpine, an Italian, commits a petty crime against an elderly Jewish grocer, Morris Bober, and his clumsy efforts to redeem his sins lead him to become the Jew's apprentice. Ultimately, he converts to Judaism and dedicates himself to leading the saint's life of the old man he has sinned against, thus assuming the legacy of Bober's own dead son. Despite the narrative contrasts to Wallant's work (which is, as well, far darker in its tone), the thematic parallels are clear, particularly in the dominant motif of the reluctant father-son relationship in both works. Like Nazerman's pawnshop, further-more, Bober's grocery store is tomblike, but it will become the womb from which new life is born. As part of his apprenticeship, Frank Alpine must learn something of the function of suffering, as the old Jew tells him with all the seasoned instinct of a prophet:

"But tell me why is it that the Jews suffer so damn much, Morris? It seems to me they like to suffer, don't they?"

"Do you like to suffer? They suffer because they are Jews."

"That's what I mean, they suffer more than they have to."

"If you live, you suffer. Some people suffer more, but not because they want. But I think if a Jew don't suffer for the Law, he will suffer for nothing."

"What do you suffer for, Morris?" Frank said.

"I suffer for you," Morris said calmly.

Frank laid his knife down on the table. His mouth ached. "What do you mean?"

"I mean you suffer for me."[2]

The dialogue is echoed in the opening and closing paragraphs of *The Pawnbroker* when an old Negro watches the pawnbroker's lonely walk along the Hudson and thinks, "That man *suffer!*" (p. 4). More pointedly, Jesus Ortiz enviously observes to his employer, "Niggers suffer like animals. They ain't caught on. Oh yeah, Jews suffer. But they do it big, they shake up the worl' with they sufferin'" (p. 27).

III   *Uses of the Literal*

Largely because of the brilliant screen version produced by Ely Landau, *The Pawnbroker* is the best known of all Wallant's writings. In its use of character, dialogue, setting, and montage techniques, the novel itself is distinctly cinematic; and in its meticulous attention to visual detail, it reminds us of Wallant's own experience as a graphic artist. In the opening pages of the novel, Wallant establishes Sol Nazerman's milieu with crisp economy by itemizing the patternless conglomeration of pawned objects which greets the pawnbroker when he opens up the shop. The same graphic precision frequently distinguishes Wallant's description of faces and gestures. Startled, Sol Nazerman stares into space, "his face seemingly caught on a shelf of ease" (p. 11). One of the pawnbroker's more regular customers, hungry for intellectual discourse, has "the face of an old Venetian doge, the features drawn with a silvery-fine pencil, the excesses reproduced in the shallowest, most subtle of creases" (p. 47). Goberman, the guilt-baiting confidence man, looks like "something just dug up and not yet shaken clean of the greyish poor soil of its recent burial" (p. 121). With comparable deftness and economy, Wallant calls forth individual settings.

Tessie's apartment house smells of garbage and soot, but her own apartment gives forth "the more personal odors of bad cooking and dust" (p. 57); the armchair into which she sinks leans "swollenly to one side under its faded cretonne covering, like an old sick elephant under shabby regal garments" (p. 58). A room in which the pawnbroker plays cards has "a damp-plush smell, like a train car opened after a long sealing" (p. 118).

Such graphic evocations of inanimate objects, as well as the tendency of metaphor to strip faces and gestures of all anthropomorphic qualities, are not merely functional in evoking visual realities. They also serve as a continual reminder of the dehumanization of the world through which the pawnbroker moves. The horrors of his past have anaesthetized him, and he views the present through the shield of his old-fashioned spectacles. But it is not only Sol Nazerman and the other survivors of holocaust who treat life in terms of bloodless, passionless commodities. Wallant presents us with a teeming host of the dispossessed—junkies, whores, petty racketeers, drifters, perverts, failures—whose sole remaining communication is dependent upon the stealing, bartering, hoarding, or pawning of inanimate objects. Thus, the black George Smith—his very name a calculated anonymity—visits Nazerman to pawn and then redeem a series of token articles and through such transactions buys precious minutes in which he can discuss Spencer and Spinoza with the former university professor. Buck White broods over schemes that will allow him to buy a Cadillac and make a renewed claim to his wife's affections, and the prostitute Mabel Wheatley coaxes presents from her customers in order to add to the hoard with which she hopes to win her young lover's affection. The racketeer Murillio accumulates third-rate works of art as though this homage to culture removes the taint from his life. A corrupt policeman attempts to barter the protection of his friendship for an electric mixer.

Again and again, Wallant shows us human relations reduced to mercantile agreements. Sol Nazerman first presumes that his contact with the social worker Marilyn Birchfield will be one of weekly payoffs. He guarantees his peace and privacy in suburban Mount Vernon by supporting his relatives there in a style to which they grow smugly accustomed. Goberman, the professional refugee, extorts money by manipulating the guilt and fear of the Jewish survivors. Until Nazerman begins the long, terrifying descent toward chaos that will culminate in his rebirth, he has never seen his "partner," Murillio, who uses the pawnshop as a front through which he can filter profits from various illegal enterprises—including the neighborhood brothel. Jesus Ortiz, inspired by legends of an enterprising uncle in Detroit, dreams the American dream of success, but a corrupted, parody-Alger version measured only by business success. At Nazerman's expense, his American "family," the Kantors, have assembled all the requisites of conspicuous-consumption success—from "the flagstone patio with its expensive, yellow-painted garden furniture" to the blandly efficient all-electric kitchen. Bertha Kantor, Nazerman's sister, has even made the ultimate transition to the WASP values of suburban America. She sits beaming at her handsome husband and daughter:

You wouldn't even guess they were Jews, Bertha thought proudly. Joan had thick, straight brown hair and even features. Her clear, shining skin was a testimonial to her mother's care and feeding, her easy smile an open proof of family love. And Selig—rosy and fair, with the same straight hair his daughter had. . . . Why, he hardly moved his hands at all, and his face was crisp with a delightfully Midwestern accent; so *American* (p. 31).

Bertha's son Morton, with the dark, morose face of a ghetto scholar, is her curse, and scarcely less alien to her dream of the Happy American Family is the heavy, brooding figure of Uncle Sol. Wallant's depiction of these latter-day melting-pot compulsions often verges on parody: Bertha Kantor is one of the least sympathetic characters the author ever created. The Kantors' social pretensions, their conspicuous consumption, the parrotings of meaningless liberal clichés, the failure of a nurturing sense of family seem yet more grotesque when, later in the novel, we are given the opportunity to contrast them with the Nazermans. The Kantor family dinner in Chapter 2 and the Nazerman family picnic recalled in Chapter 25 comprise a devastating study in comparative sociology—one made the more apt and pointed by the presence of two children in each family and the fact that both fathers are teachers. In their scramble for respectability, the Kantors have denied their origins and hence their true identity—a loss symbolized in a gesture reminiscent of *The Human Season*, when Sol drinks rootbeer from one of the *Yortzeit* glasses taken down from the kitchen cupboard.

IV   *The Man with No Allegiances*

Indeed, it is not only the Kantors who have denied their past and hence have only a spurious, synthetic existence in the present. Sol has denied his religion, his role as scholar, his emotional needs as a man. As "a man with no allegiances," he joins the living dead, and his ethical vision has become drastically foreshortened, as his thick spectacles suggest. Approached by Murillio to become a link in the chain of his illicit business enterprises, "he wasted no time worrying about the sources of money; let the Murillios of the world do what they wanted as long as they made no personal demands, as long as they left his privacy inviolate" (p. 7). In its very phrasing, the argument recalls the evasions of good German burghers who were able to ignore Nazi atrocities so long as they took place at a discrete distance. And meanwhile, as the pawnbroker, Nazerman himself becomes a parody image of the Jew as hand-rubbing Shylock: "Yes, he, Sol Nazerman, practiced the ancient, despised profession; and he survived!" (p. 8). It is, however, a form of survival that renders Nazerman machinelike, mechanical in gesture and response, and he embraces the materialist's credo with a vehemence that suggests the terrifying ruin of his spirit. Cecil Mapp, whose observation of the pawnbroker opens the novel, thinks the heavy, trudging man resembles "some kind of metal conveyance. Look like a tank or like that . . ." (p. 4). Later, Wallant extends the imagery:

He moved lumberingly, a great accumulation of strange severances, of poorly connected cogs and gears and ratchets, off balance, the imbalance overcompensated for, and so balanced again (p. 185).

Nazerman has, furthermore, sought to render the motions of mind and spirit as mechanical and passionless as those of his mutilated body. When Jesus Ortiz pleads to know the secrets of the pawnbroker's success, Nazerman declares, "I do not trust God or politics or newspapers or music or art. I do not trust smiles or clothes or buildings or scenery or smells. . . . But most of all, I do not trust people and their talk, for they have created hell with that talk . . ." (pp. 114–15). And as his young apprentice records these lessons in his heart, Nazerman announces that he only trusts money: "Next to the speed of light, which Einstein tells us is the only absolute in the universe, second only to that I would rank money. There, I have taught you the Pawnbroker's Credo, Ortiz" (p. 115).

In the scant month of the novel's action, these carefully constructed defenses will begin to crumble, and the long-buried man of feeling will be loosed from his shrouds. Nazerman grows restless and depressed, and his sleep is repeatedly visited by nightmares as the fifteenth anniversary of his family's death draws near. Most often in these dreams, but sometimes in ghastly waking reveries, the reader is made acquainted with the terrors Nazerman seeks to suppress. The scenes are relatively few, but chilling in their depiction of human degradation and loss. In the first, Nazerman's son David sinks to the floor of the densely packed cattle-car in which Jews are transported to the concentration camps and drowns in the "bottomless filth" (p. 38) there. In the next, Sol's friend Rubin, following an attempted escape, is torn apart by dogs and charred beyond recognition against an electrified fence. Later, drifting asleep while "calculating the compound interest of his savings" (p. 130), Nazerman recalls the operating room where parts were cut away from him in order to determine whether he could function without them. Following his unsuccessful confrontation with Murillio, when he is compelled to suck the barrel of a loaded gun to demonstrate his submissiveness, Nazerman dreams of the day when he was forced by a guard to study the room where Jewish women were kept for the entertainment of SS troops. There he sees his wife, Ruth, compelled to commit fellatio upon one of her captors. As his carefully built defenses erode, he dreams of his daughter Naomi impaled on a monstrous hook that pierces her body from behind and comes out her breast. Again, he sees himself digging graves for the dead and recalls the bright, glittering spectacles that tumbled at his feet when he shifted a corpse: "He put them on, and the whole vast spectacle leapt into horrid clarity" (p. 198), and he keeps them on in a self-conscious, masochistic effort to inflict on himself the total horror of this moment.

V   *Pastoral Intimations*

Ultimately, on the eve of the anniversary of his family's death, which will become the day of his own rebirth, Nazerman enters a pastoral dream of the pre-Nazi time in which he was united with his family:

He walked up the gentle slope with the jar of milk and the bottle of white wine cold and wet from the brook where he had cooled them. Butterflies anticipated his route, swirling up from the high grass in palpitating clouds of color; there was the hot, peaceful din of insects all around, a drowsy twittering of sun-weakened birds. . . . Down in the hollow, between him and the woods, his family lolled among the clover and the dandelions. His father sat against a stone in his inappropriate black suit and Yalmalka, lost in his study of a book. The children, who were trying to strip the meadow of wild flowers, paid him no attention as they crawled purposefully on their knees, the baby, Naomi, holding only a few tattered flowers, while David held his riches of yellow and pink in a thick clump. Ruth and his mother turned to him, and Ruth raised her hand in greeting. . . . Then she smiled, her teeth showing white in her dark face. . . . Her hair was a black shine of curls, and as he got closer, he saw that she had put some dandelions in it, little yellow suns in the night of her hair. . . . The children looked up, then began stumbling through the grass towards him, David with his huge clump of flowers, Naomi stumbling on her baby legs, the flowers cast down and forgotten. . . . All of them approached him with their eager smiles: his mother, his father, Ruth, the children. The humming of the bees and the flies drove happiness ever deeper into him. Their faces all came closer; he would have liked to gather them all into him, to drink them, to breathe them. And then they stopped, every blade of grass froze, each of them was arrested in motion: . . . it was like a movie which has suddenly stopped while its projecting illumination continued (pp. 241-42).

In one of the earliest lessons he gives Jesus Ortiz, the pawnbroker stresses the cliché-filled history of the myth that the Jew is alienated from the land and the cycles of nature; but in the dream-recollection of a family picnic quoted above, we see another vision, as we do in the outing with Marilyn Birchfield, when a trip up the Hudson reminds him of earlier voyages on the Vistula. Once more—as in *The Human Season*—it is the river, the lake he recalls before falling asleep, the brook in which a loving father has chilled milk and wine, that signals the character's rebirth, an event ceremonially blessed by the rain that falls outside as the pawnbroker dreams of this sunny summer day.

In the film adaptation of *The Pawnbroker*, Wallant's idyllic family outing is present throughout the film in a series of brief,

nearly subliminal cuts which gradually extend in length until the
full scene is presented. The technique (and the complementary
device whereby a crowded subway car is briefly merged in the
image of the densely packed cattle-car) is far more organic,
structurally and dramatically more compelling, than Wallant's
somewhat stilted, italicized dream sequences. The dreams occur
here with less mechanical regularity than in *The Human Season,*
yet it remains clear that Wallant lacks experience in arranging
the basic furniture of the novel. With the devices of cross-cutting
and dissolve, the filmmaker, of course, has certain obvious
narrative advantages. Furthermore, in the sequence quoted
above, Wallant can only suggest that the action slows and then
freezes, whereas director Sidney Lumet can actually film the
entire episode in slow motion. I know of no happier example of
the filmmaker's successful translation of a novelist's intention,
though with that narrative literalness which the film so often
seems to demand, the sequence is somewhat clumsily extended
to include the arrival of four Nazi soldiers, come to arrest the
family. While film, as a visual medium, must often make explicit
what is implicit and conceptual in the novel, what emanates from
the very structure of language itself, such an amendment seems
excessive. Nonetheless, other than the slight but significant
liberties taken with the novel's conclusion and an almost
inevitable oversimplification of the complex father-son motif,
the film remains a skilled and faithful adaptation of the book, in
great measure because of Rod Steiger's inspired, richly modulated interpretation of the title role.

In electing to begin his film with a brief fragment of the picnic
scene, Sidney Lumet correctly appraised its thematic significance to the novel as a whole. Like the rain which somewhat
melodramatically falls outside Nazerman's window, it testifies to
the gift of life, however atrophied, which Nazerman bears.
Wallant nudges our memory of this critical dream sequence
when, on the following anniversary morning, Nazerman looks up
to see a spastic entering his shop like "a tall marionette carved
from some black wood, his limbs controlled erratically. . . ." (p.
251). When the cripple is unable to untie the parcel he has
brought with him, Sol cuts the cord with a razor blade, to reveal
"a framed glass of brilliantly colored butterflies" (p. 251),
reminding us of those that have swirled "in palpitating clouds of
color" (p. 241) in Sol's dream. And later in the same day, through

the sacrificial death of his graceful, perplexed assistant, Sol
Nazzerman will break the spirit's sleep and rejoin the community
of suffering, grieving, celebrating man.

VI   *The Profane Priest*

Despite the pawnbroker's cold, rocklike exterior, many of his
customers see in him hope for salvation—not merely from
financial dilemmas, but from their spiritual aches and pains.
Immobile behind the grill that separates him from the public,
Nazerman resembles a priest in the confessional. Holding a silver
candelabra aloft, he resembles "a great votive statue"; the voice
in which he speaks to Jesus is a "litany"; he is privy to
"mysteries" (pp. 180–81). He protests to his brother-in-law, "I
am not your protector, nor am I your father or your doctor or
your rabbi" (p. 82), and yet those are precisely the roles he will
be compelled to play once he has confronted his authentic self.
Even when he clings with mechanical rigor to the mercantile
principles of his profession, he knows that he and his assistant, in
dealing with their customers, are "giving mercy with the backs of
their hands, touching the odd flotsam of people's lives, removing
old dreams for the loan of brief new ones . . ." (p. 105). When
two women trundle in a sewing machine to be pawned,
Nazerman briefly thinks of himself as "Solomon offering to cut
the baby in half for two warring mothers" (p. 135). Despite the
irony of such passages, the pawnbroker is at least subconsciously
aware of the destiny that makes past and present now converge
to shape his life. As he explains to Marilyn Birchfield,

"Say I am like their priest. Yes, do not be shocked, I *am*. They get as
much from me as they do from their churches. They bring me their
troubles in the shapes of old table radios and watches and stolen
typewriters and gold-plated crucifixes and half-paid-for cameras. And
I, I give them absolution in hard cash. . . . Oh yes, they know I only
give a small fraction of what the thing is worth. But what they get is still
a prize to them. They know how difficult it is to get *anything* from me.
If I were to soften up, I would devaluate their little triumphs. They
would be shocked and confused; I would be like a priest giving in to
temptation" (pp. 143–44).

The self-deprecation, the near-contempt, with which Nazerman
presents this argument is one of the final and most pathetic

defenses he makes in the course of the novel; in thus anatomizing his wordly vocation, he ironically points toward the spiritual vocation he must inevitably assume. His very name makes that vocation palpable. As "Sol," or sun god, he lends life and energy to his customers, his assistant, his adopted family, and to his fellow Jewish survivors. If we hear in his name an echo of the biblical Saul, first king of Israel, we should remember that both Saul and Sol had sons named David and that from King David's progeny was born the Messiah. If the name Sol is short for "Solomon," the allusion is not merely to the renowned justice of the Hebrew king, ironically recalled in the episode of the sewing machine, but to the literal translation of the Hebrew name: peace. The pawnbroker's last name, Nazerman, is suggestive of Nazereth and the Nazarene. The meaning inherent in such names will finally be decoded by the delicate, fatherless boy, Jesus Ortiz.

So intense and, ultimately, so traumatic is the confrontation of father with surrogate son that it is likely to overshadow other events in the novel that help prompt the spasms of rebirth we see in the conclusion of *The Pawnbroker*. In the bribe-taking Jewish policeman, Leventhal, Sol Nazerman finds a clownish parody of his own corruption, for Leventhal is also on Murillio's payroll; his reiterated greeting of "landsman" underscores the pawnbroker's loss of real community. Similarly, George Smith's hunger for intellectual discourse reminds the pawnbroker of his own forsaken career. When he attacks the cringing Goberman as "a professional sufferer, a practicing refugee," and a man who "cannot sleep too well" (p. 124), he might be addressing himself in a mirror. And Nazerman finds the echo of his own corruption in Murillio who, like the Nazi surgeons, threatens the protesting Jew with castration, and gazes at him, "his lids . . . lowered so his eyes seem heavy and toxic" (p. 161).

Each of these confrontations helps to dislodge the stone from the tomb of Nazerman's heart, though of all the minor characters it is Marilyn Birchfield who in her naive exuberance for life suggests the possibility of salvation. She flaunts health "in her even smile," and her healing association with nature is outlined in her name. It is in her company that the pawnbroker sees the polluted water of the Hudson transformed by an "illusion of brightness," and that he has a vision, so reminiscent of *The Human Season,* of "the half-naked bodies of the boys across the

river as they splashed into the water and then climbed back up
the coal chute like gleaming, newly caught fish" (p. 144). Later,
during their river outing, he is first able to confront memories of
the past outside his dreams, and to imagine a destiny other than
the one to which he has condemned himself. Wallant underscores the regenerative aspects of nature through allusions to
Chekhov's "A Day in the Country," a favorite story of both
Nazerman and Marilyn Birchfield. Chekhov pays a moving
tribute to the simple people who have learned "not from books,
but in the fields, in the wood, on the riverbank,"[3] and while their
knowledge cannot erase the injustices of the world, it can help to
ease the painful loneliness of two orphaned children. In refusing
to share such knowledge with his "orphaned" assistant, Nazerman commits yet another crime against nature.

The inexplicable pain which the pawnbroker feels inside, and
which he at one point ironically describes as a "tumor," is the
inevitable agony resulting from the death of the old self. Though
he yearns for nothingness, "in the part of him not apparent there
[is] still darkness and terrifying growth" (p. 111). Far from being
the tumor with which Nazerman could reckon as simple physical
violation, the pain springs from more complex sources: "he felt
pain, deep inside him, a growth slowly extending to pierce him,
to meet the stabs from people outside himself, people who would
raise their hands to him" (p. 167). When he suspects Jesus of
scheming against him, the revelation briefly pierces his
indifference, and he stands swaying "in front of the window like
a plaintiff at the Wailing Wall" (p. 186), a foreshadowing of the
tears that he will shed in the conclusion of the novel. Deluding
himself that he perhaps has, after all, only "some minor disease,"
Nazerman compares himself to Eliot's Prufrock, and recalls the
lines "I grow old . . . I grow old . . . / I shall wear the bottoms
of my trousers rolled."[4] The allusion to J. Alfred Prufrock, whose
nervously contrived indifference so remorselessly estranges him
from life, stresses Nazerman's affinities to the host of lonely,
anguished men who populate the modern literary imagination.
Perhaps even more illuminating, however, is the passage from
Dante with which Eliot prefaces his poem:

> S'io credesse che mia reposta fosse
> A persona che mai tornasse al mondo,
> Questa fiamma staria senza piu scosse.

Ma Perciocche giammai di questo fondo
Non torno vivo alcun, s'i'odo il vero,
Senza tema d'infamia ti rispondo.[5]

As in Eliot's poem we are taken on a guided tour of a
contemporary hell—not merely that of Nazi atrocities, but the
meaner, more insidious inferno which man builds within himself.
In its imagery, Wallant's novel also owes a debt to Eliot's *The
Waste Land*. The pawnshop, Tessie's apartment, Murillio's rooms
are all described as dry and dusty, and there is a curse on
Nazerman, the Fisher King. Of the grotesques who parade
through the pawnshop one might well say, as Eliot says of the
crowds pouring over London Bridge, "I had not thought death
had undone so many."[6] It is partly through the laying on of hands
by a pure woman, Marilyn Birchfield, that the king is healed, and
spiritual regeneration is signaled by the drenching rain that falls
on the night before Nazerman's resurrection.

VII   *A Strangely Matched Team*

In the relationship of Nazerman and Jesus, teacher and
apprentice, Wallant reiterates his central theme of the relationship between father and son. Jesus is obsessed by the mystery of
the pawnbroker—not merely the secrets of his commercial
success, but the meaning of the crudely tattooed numbers on his
arm which suggest an exalted secret society, the withdrawn,
distracted look on his face that comes from the contemplation of
hidden wisdom. Significantly, Jesus is fatherless, beset by "a
deep-rooted nervousness . . . , a feeling of fragility and terror"
(p. 9) that comes from haunted memories he struggles to
suppress. A group of white boys once threatened to emasculate
him, as Nazi doctors threatened to emasculate Nazerman.
Wallant emphasizes the bizarre kinship of Jesus and the Nazerman when he describes them as "a strangely matched team
engaged in an even stranger performance" (p. 105). Kneeling
before the crucifix, Jesus often imagines the bearded figure
there to be "the father he had never seen. . . ." Later, his
apprenticeship nearly complete, he sees the same figure as
Nazerman himself. It is only on the perfunctory surface of shop-
talk and recitations of the Pawnbroker's Credo that the
relationship of Sol and Jesus is a materialist one. Beneath the

surface it is awash with the unspoken cries of the heart, with the need for personal, moral, paternal recognition. At moments the pawnbroker senses this deeper relationship, seeing Jesus's "unnerving quality of volatile innocence," his perturbing "cleanness of spirit," but he will ultimately betray the lonely yearning of this fatherless boy by bequeathing him only his own most cynical, pessimistic vision. It is on the basis of such "knowledge" that, in a cafeteria facing the Tabernacle of Jesus Our Lord, his assistant plots the robbery of the pawnshop.

In attempting to prove to the pawnbroker that he is worthy of learning the cabalistic secrets of his profession, Jesus Ortiz describes a rich uncle in Detroit who runs a clothing business that has earned him wealth and respectability. Jesus takes pride and substance from that success, which has planted the first seed for his own success dream. Sol Nazerman, as "uncle," plays a similar role for the Kantors, and indeed the dispirited blacks who visit his shop address him as "uncle." In refusing to see these parallels between his life and that of the young Jesus, Nazerman gives further evidence of his blindness. Wallant's imagery repeatedly underscores the pawnbroker's lack of vision in references to "his eyes lidded with boredom," "his glass-covered eyes," his "staring out sightlessly through the glass like some exhibited creature from another clime," "his face sightless" when he answers questions, his "eyes blind" as he gazes "myopically" at the cafeteria in which he sits before his interview with Murillio, the *"triumph of blindness"* when he refuses to acknowledge the forgiveness in his wife's tears, "the round, old-fashioned spectacles" he borrows from the dead, the gentleness that infuses his face when he removes his glasses to reminisce about his childhood with Marilyn Birchfield. On the hot September day that precedes his anniversary, Nazerman stands behind the pawnshop counter in a near-trance, and "the eyes behind the weird glasses were larger and darker, brooding and full of a melancholy so profound that it almost seemed to emit a sound . . ." (p. 277). When the shot is fired that kills Jesus, Wallant notes that Nazerman "was blinded, saw only smoke." Later, restored to life and to grief, he is blinded only by his own tears: "And when he tried to wipe his eyes, indeed, cleared them momentarily, he saw the ineffable marvel of their eyes and skins" (p. 133).

VIII   *A Shadow on the Soul*

The pawnbroker's quaint, old-fashioned spectacles may not literally be the same as those "round, old-fashioned" ones he took from the corpse he once buried, but figuratively they are. Seeing the world only in terms of the holocaust he survived, he must inevitably judge it wrongly, lead his apprentice astray, betray the trust that is given him, desecrate the symbol of his holy calling. He ignores Jesus's plea for help as he does that of his rejected nephew Morton, as he had once shut his ears to his own drowning son, David. The full horror of Sol Nazerman's dehumanization is first revealed to him when he learns that the money he handles for Murillio probably comes from the brothel he operates and that he can no more remain indifferent to this exploitation than he could to the Nazi brothel in which his wife was imprisoned. Jesus Ortiz, seeking to boost his masculine image with his prostitute girl friend by linking himself to the pawnbroker's profession, ironically underscores the inhumanity of Nazerman's philosophy.

"Nazerman say to me one day, 'You know how old this profession is?' . . . And he say *thousands of years.* He say one time the Babylon . . . some crazy tribe, they use to take crops and even people for pawn. A man make loans on his family—wife, kid, anything. I mean you see what a solid business that is—thousands of years" (p. 71).

But far from being cheered by this historical justification, Jesus can only think despondently of "the succession of rooms he had lived in" and "a thousand times multiplied, those few times his name had been doubted, his paternity jeered at" (p. 71).

The inevitable outcome of the confusion of values, the cynicism and self-doubt that Nazerman has planted in Jesus Ortiz's already troubled spirit is the robbery which gives the novel its dramatic (but not thematic) conclusion. The entire scene has an almost surrealistically distorted quality. It is the dreaded day of Nazerman's anniversary, of his final showdown with Murillio, and through the store moves a parade of grotesques reminiscent of Nathanael West's *Miss Lonelyhearts,* another novel in which a reluctant Christ is compelled to embrace his true vocation. Sol first greets the spastic lepidopterist, next a voiceless man whose lower jaw is "a gaping, wet

redness," a cadaverous young woman, and then an entire chorus
of the damned that moves before him like an Hieronymous Bosch
fantasy cursed into life, until the pawnbroker "stretched on the
rack of his sight and smell and hearing, saw all the naked souls
ready to spill blood on him" (p. 257).

Sol Nazerman has survived, has defended his privacy, by
inuring himself to the ugliness and pain that fill this ghetto
world; the word "stone" or "stone-like" is used repeatedly to
describe his calculated immunity. But like Miss Lonelyhearts he
will at last be compelled to dream "the Christ dream." As the
crowd of pilgrims disperses and Jesus disappears into the loft
overhead, Nazerman notes that the store seems "a peculiar and
grotesque tomb." Irrelevantly, he picks up a feather-duster and
begins to flick at the merchandise "like some devout witch-
doctor" (p. 263), feeling all the while "the heatless press of the
grave" (p. 264). And as life falls "like a shadow on his soul" (p.
265), Jesus's three confederates enter the store, dressed in
bizarre Halloween masks. With the feather-duster still absurdly
clutched in his hand, Nazerman resists the robbers, inviting the
death God has denied him. Robinson raises a gun and points it at
the pawnbroker, and as he pulls the trigger, Jesus throws himself
in the path of the bullet. Clutching the boy's body, Nazerman
thinks, "Oh to see, to know!" (p. 270) and as Jesus dies in his
arms, the pawnbroker feels "full of the flow of some great
wound" (p. 272). In the agonizing minutes that follow, he
becomes aware of the sound of weeping, "growing louder and
louder and louder, filling the Pawnbroker's ears, flooding him,
drowning him, dragging him back to that sea of tears he had
thought to have escaped" (p. 272). The weeping is his own, the
tears the ones he could not shed when he smelled the burning
flesh of the concentration camp ovens: *"None of it brought a tear
to his eyes, and his eyes became burning hot balls in the flesh of
his face" (p. 225).* And in this baptism of tears, foreshadowed by
images of brook, river, lake, and rain, "all his anaesthetic
numbness left him. He became terrified of the touch of air on
raw wounds" (p. 272). Like the electric shock which sears not
merely the body but the soul of Joe Berman, the gunshot that
kills Jesus Ortiz precipitates the pawnbroker back into life.
Where he was once repulsed by the smells and shabbiness of his
clients, he is now aware of "the crush of warm bodies" (p. 273),
and he will soon recognize their "ineffable marvel."

IX *Recognitions*

In the hours that follow Jesus's death, three critical events occur which give the novel its thematic resolution. First, Nazerman telephones his nephew Morton, who has so long adored his strange, moody uncle, and like Jesus Ortiz sought in him the comfort and the teachings of a father. When he describes what has occurred in the pawnshop, he significantly says, "My boy, my assistant, has been killed . . ." (p. 274), and the words "my boy" are the belated recognition Jesus had craved. With a new humility, Sol is able to say to his nephew, "I *need* you, Morton," and when Morton replies, "You'll have to teach me" (p. 275), we have the promise that this second apprenticeship will be very different from the first. Following the telephone call, Sol Nazerman sleeps and dreams a dream totally lacking "the usual horror." In it he approaches a ruined, deserted concentration camp in company with his nephew and his friend Tessie Rubin. The black-uniformed guard who greets them is Murillio, and he reads to Nazerman from a slip of paper: *"Your dead are not buried here."* It is the same lesson read him by the black mother struggling with all her will to maintain the dignity of her family: "You an' me both know what you bury might jus' as well stay dead," but Nazerman could not accept her words until Jesus Ortiz sacrificed his life.

In the third and most significant of these near-ritual acts of atonement (at-*one*-ment), Nazerman begins "the long, underground journey to Tessie's house, to help her mourn" (p. 279). Like the affirmation of Berman's decision to help his daughter mourn, this single act is eloquent demonstration of reunion with the community of man. Earlier in the novel, following the death of her father, Tessie has accused Nazerman of being inhuman. "What would you have me say or do?" he asks, and her broken answer is, "I don't know . . . with me perhaps. . . ." What Tessie seeks to articulate here is the disgrace of the old man lying dead with no one to pray for him. "Won't you even come to the . . . funeral?" Tessie asks, and when Nazerman refuses she murmurs, "Go then, leave me. I can mourn alone" (pp. 230-31). This major sign of Nazerman's own rebirth was absent from Wallant's original chapter outline for *The Pawnbroker*, as was his telephone call to his nephew Morton. In comparison with the author's original scheme, the reader realizes yet more fully the

richness of the final draft of the novel. Following the death of
Jesus Ortiz, the following episodes are outlined:

Chapter 19
It is the next day. The naked pain of love is out like a killing growth
on Sol Nazerman. He goes with Marilyn Birchfield and the prostitute to
the funeral. The grief-stricken mother accuses him. He tells her with a
sense of wonder and bewilderment that he loved him, that he loves all
of them.

Chapter 20
He wakes from one of his terrible dreams calmly, almost stoically. I
am alive, it must be enough. He calls the racketeer and tells him off.
Then he waits calmly for Murillio and his men. They come and the
racketeer admits defeat.
Later he talks to Marilyn Birchfield and tells her with gentle regret
that there can be nothing for there are too many things between them,
his dream alone being more than she could ever surmount.
The last scene shows him walking along the river, heading for his car.
He has a strange gentle look on his face. The plasterer and the old
janitor talk of him. The janitor quotes from the bible. The plasterer just
says compassionately, suddenly touched by a tiny flicker of love
because he is able to pity someone else for once, "That man
suffer. . . ."[7]

The character of Tessie does not exist in this detailed description
of the novel, and the time-scheme Wallant had envisioned is
clearly less effective than the one he ultimately chose. The
confrontation with Murillio, the death of Jesus, the final "stoic"
dream all occur on the day of his tragic anniversary. So too,
significantly, does his decision to join Tessie in her mourning.
The film version of the novel entirely misses the resonance of
this final moment, for in the last scene the pawnbroker is seen
approaching the subway, in a long shot that loses him in the
jostling, undifferentiated mob. One also loses the lyricism of his
vision of the river, the strength of his resolution to "accept the
pain of it, if not happily, like a martyr, at least willingly, like an
heir." Furthermore, Lumet's decision to show Nazerman turn
from the body of Jesus and impale his hand on a paper spike
seems not only a gratuitous emendation, but a symbolic
manipulation in itself more embarrassing than Wallant in his least
controlled, most self-conscious moments.

If Sol Nazerman's story often parallels that of Joe Berman in the shared inability to cope with emotional loss, properly and finally to mourn the dead and to build a new life in the present, there is a further and more chilling parallel which, in both instances, may be a major cause of this emotional paralysis. Like Berman, Nazerman has "sinned" against his own son. In his nightmare he recalls how he and his family were packed into the cattle-car, locked in place by the pressure of two hundred other bodies. Nazerman studies the landscape that passes by outside, distracting himself from the voice of his young son, who pleads that he is slipping in the filth that litters the floor. His wife, Ruth, begs Sol to save the boy, but *"just moving his nose down an inch toward the carpeting of feces nauseated Sol. The child would turn his insides out"* (p. 38). When he complains that he can't move to reach the boy, he does so "peevishly, " and confronted by his wife's grim face he shouts, "I can do nothing . . . I am helpless, do you hear?" (p. 38). But his voice is "dispassionate, soulless," and his son drowns at his feet. Yet it is not the physical near-impossibility of saving the child that makes Nazerman helpless; it is (and here the contrast with Berman is noteworthy) also the fastidiousness of the intellectual bourgeois who would prefer not to dirty his hands: *"The child would turn his insides out."* Only if we understand the full horror of this crime against both nature and nurture can we fully comprehend the conclusion of the brothel scene which Nazerman witnesses, when the SS trooper pulls Ruth to her knees and forces her head between his legs, just as she recognizes her husband:

. . . *from that hideously obscene position, pierced so vilely, she endured the zenith of her agony and was able to pass through it. Until finally she was able to award him the tears of forgiveness. But he was not worthy of her award and took the infinitely meaner triumph of blindness* . . . (p. 169).

It is not merely for his witnessing of her shame that Ruth forgives Sol, but for the death of their son, and the blindness with which he greets her award will destroy his spiritual son Jesus, though there is still hope of salvation for his adoring, persecuted nephew with his brooding ghetto-scholar's face.[8]

The Pawnbroker is Wallant's darkest, most Dostoevskian work, yet the writing of it seems to have liberated the novelist's spirit,

to have released the magnificent comic voice which rings
through *The Children at the Gate, The Tenants of Moonbloom*,
and his incomplete last novel, *Tannenbaum's Journey*. As in *The
Human Season*, Wallant densely mingles Jewish and Christian
motifs, but often so self-consciously that at critical moments
allegory threatens to overwhelm the novel's dramatic structure
and its inspired compassion veers toward bathos. Ultimately, it is
the precision and majesty of language itself which transforms a
contrived, symbol-ridden narrative into a literary document of
such profound and memorable consequence.

CHAPTER 6

The Children at the Gate

I *The Dilemma of Mixed Allegiance*

The Children at the Gate clearly played a special role in Wallant's creative imagination, for the novel exists in two distinct manuscript versions and a third draft filled with handwritten revisions; at the end of his life the author made plans to dramatize the work. Only two weeks before his death, he drew a rough sketch of a stage-set for the play on a page of the Sunday *New York Times* (November 15, 1962). It shows, at stage rear, six individual rooms, on two levels—four of them containing hospital beds, the others no doubt intended to represent office and waiting room. On the apron of the stage, wheelchairs are clustered, and here the solarium scenes of Angelo's mystified encounters with the tragic-clown Sammy would have taken place. A catwalk extends over the first rows of the audience—perhaps to serve for Angelo's entrances from the drugstore across the way. A few hastily drawn lines seem to suggest the presence of musicians in the orchestra pit, as though the author were perhaps toying with the idea of a musical version of his work.

With fitting irony, the page on which Wallant makes this sketch contains the following words, framed by a black box: "RACE, HUMAN. Beloved father of science and technology, adored mother of arts and culture. Departed this earth suddenly, but not without warning. Survived by no one."

Though Wallant's concept of the novel was to undergo major alterations between the first and second drafts, the conflict between scientific-technological values and spiritual-humanistic ones is explored in both versions. In the summer of 1961, when

91

he applied for a Guggenheim Fellowship, he outlined the
concerns that would shape his next novel:

> It has always seemed to me that one of man's most chronic conflicts
> and perhaps the one with which he can least come to terms, is that
> struggle, within himself, which divides him between rationality and
> mysticism. I believe that—no matter what things we come to learn
> scientifically—we must accept as a concurrent phenomenon that
> immense and dimly shaped world that exists outside the calculable one.
> The so-called "factual" truths we have learned as a species have
> indeed advanced us in many obvious ways, and yet are we not still
> insane children hastening toward our own extinction because we have
> struggled to extinguish those vast, elemental urges which argue for
> perpetuity, which ultimately affirm life itself? We have discovered
> complexities of language, words with which we are able to manage the
> hideous toys of our technological "progress." It is the artificial and
> hectic brilliance of our language which has dimmed our view of what
> life is really about. . . .
> I do not advocate a return to ignorance, nor do I bemoan man's
> literacy or his ability to make the world more habitable. I am exalted by
> his ability to find beauty and his talent for exploiting the limitless
> phenomena within his imagination. Only I deplore the arrogance that
> has cost him his ability to wonder, the facile learning that has deprived
> him of the humility that would allow him to accept his small place in
> the infinite. I believe this arrogance, born of technological virtuosity,
> threatens to "put him out" like the tiny match flame he is.
> I do not pick one type of truth over the other. I admit the logic of
> evolution, and I accept the scientific truths I have learned. Only I am
> convinced that man must inhabit two worlds. To describe the two
> worlds we use words such as "Intellect vs. Emotion"; or even more
> subjectively "cold and warm," depending upon the geography of our
> own personalities. The vocabulary is arbitrary, but the truth of man's
> dual citizenship is not. We *do* dwell in concentric perceptual circles. It
> seems to me that only in creating a peaceful co-existence between the
> levels of existence can man survive. I have directed all the force of my
> writing toward this because of my own pre-occupation with this
> universal dilemma of mixed allegiance.
> In this, my third novel, I would hope to illumine another small area of
> this gigantic human disturbance.

At the time he prepared this statement as part of his
Guggenheim application, Wallant had almost certainly com-
pleted the first draft of the novel that would become *The
Children at the Gate;* though the theme of "Intellect vs.

Emotion" plays a role in the earlier version, it is far more richly articulated in the manuscript which Wallant gave his publisher before departing for Europe in the spring of 1962. One should note Wallant's reference to "my own preoccupation with this universal dilemma of mixed allegiance." Only a few years before, Wallant had seen his writing and his painting as avocations— perhaps as release from the routine assignments he handled as an advertising art director—and not ones which in any way conflicted with the requirements of his bread-and-butter career. By the summer of 1961, however, he has come to think of himself as a novelist, so that his own allegiances are in conflict as never before. In the months following submission of his application, and well before he was informed of his success, he dedicated himself to his writing with unparalleled intensity, producing not only the second version of *The Children at the Gate* but a finished manuscript of *The Pawnbroker*—both in little more than six months.

II   *View of a Marvelous City*

There are numerous parallels, in both action and characterization, between the two versions of what Wallant called "the Sammy novel." Both concern the relationship between a skeptical, literal-minded man and a tender-hearted clownish Jew named Sammy. In both, a little girl name Maria Alvarez is raped by a Russian immigrant named Lebedov, and Sammy is for a time suspected of the crime. Released from prison, he pleads for the Russian's forgiveness, and is martyred for his efforts. As a symbol of the spiritual legacy he leaves behind, of the new life his martyrdom has made possible for his friend, Sammy leaves him a small insurance policy.

Wallant originally entitled his novel *A Many-Storied City*, but altered the title to *View of a Marvelous City*. In this version, Sammy's friend is a forty-three-year-old Negro, a semi-alcoholic who was once a teacher but now works in a dime store and occasionally types theses for university students. Ben Kellogg (the name is later altered to Ben Myer) spends much of his free time with Sammy Aaronsohn, who occupies the shabby apartment house. Sammy is a lean, aged-looking Jew with a great love and natural understanding for children. In a world where gestures of affection are clumsily rare, Sammy's obvious

adoration inevitably arouses suspicion. Other tenants of the slum
neighborhood include Lebedov, a ragman who frequently beats
his wife, the Alvarez family, and a fastidious young man named
Howard Miller, who reappears as a homosexual orderly in *The
Children at the Gate*. In his description of Howard, sitting in the
neighborhood bar where much of the novel's action takes place,
Wallant shows the deftness for minor character portraits that
was to animate *The Tenants of Moonbloom:*

> In a booth near the bar, Howard sat, sipping a Manhattan and reading a
> book. His tie was still snug, his shirt hardly wrinkled, as though it
> covered some cool wooden body that gave out no heat. From time to
> time he worked his neck upward in a twisting motion, something like a
> cork being coaxed out of the neck of a bottle.

Sammy is fascinated by Howard, as he is by all the lost, lonely,
displaced souls clustered in this decaying neighborhood, and he
thinks, ironically, of writing a book about them all—in which
case it would have to be *Crime and Punishment* or *The Divine
Comedy*. Because no one has ever taken his compassion, his
yearning, or his lust seriously, Sammy has become a clown in self-
defense, but he seems less content with the role than in the
second version of the novel, for he greedily saves his money with
the goal of starting a new life as a teacher.

Wallant's theme of the conflict between intellect and emotion
is illustrated in *The Children at the Gate* not merely through the
contrasting characters of Angelo and his friend Sammy, but also
through the two hospitals—one old, inefficient, but somehow
softened and humanized by its very dilapidations, and the other
the gleaming alabaster sheath of the high-rise, superefficient
technological masterpiece that rises nearby. Wallant's argument
is clear: like John Updike in *The Poorhouse Fair*, he distrusts a
system which sanctifies efficiency and physical comfort while
denying the emotional and spiritual deprivations offman. In *View
of a Marvelous City* a similar contrast is present. In the old,
decaying neighborhood where Ben and Sammy live there still
exists a sense of polyglot community—the very air is filled with
human voices, all expressing their joys and pains in a variety of
accents, but the neighborhood will soon disintegrate under the
wrecker's ball.

The dehumanized technological landscape urgently needs the

message of compassion which Sammy brings, and his friend Ben Kellogg vaguely understands this, but as in *The Children at the Gate,* this apostle will betray his savior. When Sammy is arrested on suspicion after the Alvarez girl disappears, Ben wanders the streets, trying to persuade himself that he is not responsible for Sammy, that Sammy is insane, that he means nothing to him, that he means everything. Ultimately, he goes to the police to inform them that Sammy was once picked up on suspicion of immoral behavior with a young boy. And then comes the surprise of Lebedov's confession of guilt, made in both versions of the novel to Sammy's reluctant apprentice. Sammy emerges from imprisonment in a state of shock, having so keenly felt the treatment he received that he can identify with both the murdered and the murderer:

"I began to know what the murdered would feel because I felt it all. And because I felt it all, I was the murderer. It seemed very simple to me. I never felt anything so bad; I can't describe. My whole life was like a nightmare. How can I say . . . like I was so lonely. . . . After a while it seemed simpler not to argue with them. It seemed I was the murderer. I saw her all bloody and ruined and I was the one, in my brain I was the one. Maybe I had thought things like that, maybe I could have done it. And I felt like I did. So how much worse could it be? And you know, Ben, I don't feel any different now, no different. What am I going to do about that?"

What Sammy does is to plead for forgiveness of Lebedov, simultaneously recalling the forgiveness he never received from his own judgmental rabbi father; and in doing so, Sammy is transformed from clown to saint. *View of a Marvelous City* is thus much more Sammy's story than Ben's, though Ben is the ultimate inheritor of Sammy's catechism of love.

III   *Wandering Jew and Worker Priest*

In rewriting the novel, Wallant makes Sammy both more enigmatic and more robustly comic, but at the same time he lays greater stress on Sammy's friend, the young Italian boy with "the dedicated look of a worker priest" (p. 6) whose life is so profoundly, traumatically altered by the death of the Jewish hospital orderly. Wallant first entitled this revised novel *Sammy and Angelo,* then *Angelo and the Wandering Jew,* then *In the Time of Sammy,* and borrowed the final title from T. S. Eliot's *Ash Wednesday:*.

> Will the veiled sister pray for
> Those who walk in darkness, who chose thee
>   and oppose thee,
> Those who are torn on the horn between
>   season and season,
>   time and time, between
> Hour and hour, word and word, power and power,
>   those who wait
> In darkness? Will the veiled sister pray
> For children at the gate
> Who will not go away and cannot pray:
> Pray for those who chose and oppose
>
>   O my people, what have I done unto thee.[1]

Eliot's poem describes successive stages in the spiritual experience of a man at peace neither with the real world nor with any concept of afterlife or of transcendent value. This troubled seeker moves from despair to self-abnegation, sorrow, moral awakening, faith, the hunger for grace, and, in the closing lines of the poem, to renewal of his long-dead yearning for both God and the world. In the section of *Ash Wednesday* from which Wallant draws the novel's eipgraph, a veiled sister moves through a grove of "eternal dolor," and the anguished speaker wonders if she will pray for "those who offend her"—a passage which directly recalls Angelo's conflict with the troubled Sister Louise. Sister Louise is, in turn, counterpointed by all the voiceless plaster and cement Madonnas who oversee Angelo's journey. Just as Eliot's sere landscape holds within it a promise of the restoration of the Garden, so Sammy remarks, " 'It's a beginning. If I keep going I may bring back *Gahn Eydem.*' He laughed at Angelo's puzzled expression. 'The Garden of Eden— Paradise!' " (p. 150). If there is, here, no Veiled Lady to plead for the innocent children who cluster at the gate, Sammy will pray for them all, as he literally does when he takes over the hospital's intercom system to recite the Kaddish. Wallant could hardly be said to owe his theme of regeneration to Eliot's poem, for it is the consistent subject of all his published novels, but knowledge of

Eliot's work no doubt plays a role in the intensification of religious allusion and of myth structures in the final version of *The Children at the Gate.*

As in *The Pawnbroker,* Wallant has created a master-apprentice situation in which the older man is a Jew, the younger a Catholic, but in this case the burden of cynicism, the pose of rational detachment, is given to the younger man, and it is the older Jew who is finally martyred. The crucial decision to change the apprentice from a black to an Italian may have come about because Wallant had already so intensively explored the black-white relationship in *The Pawnbroker;* one should note, however, that the pairing in *View of a Marvelous City* is strikingly different from that in *The Pawnbroker,* and that it in fact anticipates Bernard Malamud's treatment of the conflict between black and Jewish identity in *The Tenants.* But perhaps Wallant simply understood too little of the problems of black Americans, for the portrait of Ben Kellogg as a defeated alcoholic often seems lifeless and contrived. Furthermore, in his previous novels the author had endowed older men with the promise of new life, while in his later works the heroes become younger, more supple, more capable of living out that promise. Hence, his hero becomes a scrawny, cynical, nineteen-year-old Italian boy named Angelo DeMarco. Brooding, humorless, Angelo is almost obsessively devoted to an empirical, rational world-view. From the pathetically small legacy of his father, he cherishes a "thin, gray, austere volume" entitled *A Child's Book of Natural Science,* and he has used it as inspiration for his literalist faith:

It had unlocked a landscape for him, and he left it now in honorable pasture, a child's book, but father to all the rest—to the books of astronomy, zoology, physics, and chemistry, and the scrapbook with clippings on scientific subjects from magazines and newspapers (p. 5).

Angelo clings desperately to the rationalist panacea as a defense against the horrors of his life—a loveless, fatherless home, the hypocrisy of the church, an idiot sister, a tryannical uncle, a mother wasted by self-pity and religious obsession, the dying patients he visits twice daily in his rounds of the hospital. But Angelo, as his very name suggests, has a profound capacity for spiritual change and redemption—one that will finally be

released by the dialectical tension of the novel, by his reluctant
brotherhood with the Jewish Quixote, Samuel Abel Cahan.

IV *Jewish and Christian Metaphor*

As in his previous novels, Wallant evokes biblical parallels in
order to lend resonance to character and theme, without pushing
his allusions toward the neat patterns of allegory. Once more,
Jewish (Old Testament) and Christian (New Testament) characters confront one another—as do Jewish and Christian myth and
metaphor; the result is a kind of ecumenical fusion which
underscores the fundamental spiritual impulses out of which the
novel is written. *The Children at the Gate* alludes to both the
Cain and Abel story and the story of the life of Christ, with
particular stress on the Savior's betrayal and crucifixion. "Abel"
in Hebrew means "transitoriness," and there is, indeed, something fleeting, even ghostly, about each of Sammy's entrances
and exits in the novel. The biblical Abel is murdered by Cain,
who is cursed and condemned to the suffering which is life, sent
forth to wander the earth East of Eden. Similarly, Angelo
DeMarco is "marked" by his betrayal of Sammy, and sets off on
his travels at the conclusion of the novel. The brotherhood of the
two characters is underscored by the fact that both are
fatherless; as Sammy remarks near the conclusion of the novel,
". . . I guess you would say we were all orphans together" (p.
150). If there is, in the relationship, the occasional suggestion
that Angelo as spiritual apprentice finds a surrogate father in
Sammy, the motif of fraternity is yet stronger. Interconnected
with the Cain-Abel allusions are references to the life of Christ.
Sammy's first name recalls the biblical Samuel—the "name of
God" and the one "heard of God"—and his last, Cahan,
translates from the Hebrew "Kahan" with the phrase "to act as a
priest." Last of the judges and first of the prophets in the Old
Testament, it is Samuel who persuades the nation of Israel to
abandon idolatry; it is he who anoints Saul as the first King of
Israel, then reproves him and anoints David, who founds the line
into which Christ is born.[2]
    Not merely do his names suggest links between Old Testament
and New, but many of Sammy's actions will consciously parody
the miracles of Christ. When Angelo encounters him swabbing
the floor of the emergency room, a cover for another drug-

stealing raid, he accuses the Jewish orderly of not showing proper reverence for his job. "No, no, just the opposite, just the opposite," Sammy answers. "In fact I was acting out one of the miracles" (p. 47). And when Angelo takes him up with the question "Which one was that?" Sammy lifts first one foot and then the other out of the water on the floor and replies, "What else?. . . Walking on the water" (p. 47). During one of their clandestine solarium dinners, he reenacts the miracle of the loaves and the fishes: "Now observe, out of nowhere—*poof*—a fish dinner!" (p. 83) Later, Sammy tempts Angelo into trying to wake the dead, jokes about the vagueness of his own birthday, the mystery of his ancestry, and regales him with contemporary parables of love, anguish, and heroism; he confesses to Angelo that he has "never, never touched a woman in my whole life" (p. 160); and his tender, protective relationship to the children in the hospital is an echo of Jesus' words, "Suffer little children, and forbid them not, to come unto me: for of such is the kingdom of heaven." Like Christ, Sammy will be betrayed by one of his "disciples," and in parody of the crucifixion, immolated on the pickets of an iron fence.

V   The Assaults of Birth and Extinction

The dedication to an essentially spiritual vision of experience, to which Berman and Nazerman come only after long suffering, seems to be Sammy's messianic birthright. As a hospital orderly, he has ample occasion to express his philosophy of love—even though his concern for human suffering will lead him to such questionable extremes as stealing drugs to administer to patients unable to bear their pain, a transgression for which Angelo will betray his brother in an anonymous note to the hospital authorities. The hospital setting is important, and far more suggestive than the rooming house of *View of a Marvelous City*, for it shows the inadequacy of modern technology to treat the deeper ills of man; and, since it is a Catholic hospital, the failure of institutionalized religion is also implied. The motif is made yet stronger in the gleaming white specter of the new hospital which rises nearby:

Angelo fixed hard on what *was,* and stared at the beacon light on the new building, seeing faintly its immense, pale shape against the dark sky.

"It looks like a tombstone or a factory," Sammy said, following his gaze. "Too cold-looking, got no character" (p. 55).

Angelo's job as general factotum in his uncle's pharmacy gives him at least a tentative link to this world of scientific "progress," though its rationality is undercut by Frank DeMarco's home-brewed medicines ["Medicine helps people if they think it helps them" (p. 14)] and the fact that, apart from his hospital rounds, Angelo's duties seem to center on the soda fountain. But he compulsively reads his scientific texts in order to sustain at least the veneer of rational detachment that shields him from the pain and suffering he sees all about him, little realizing that his actions are as self-delusive as the religious pieties and rituals which he despises. Here, as in all of Wallant's work, the lost and tormented turn to fetishes as a narcotic for their pain. Hence, Angelo's mother fills the house with the clutter of her tormented faith:

There were pictures of saints and Madonnas, some of them small reproductions of Renaissance paintings, others like sentimental bubble-gum cards. There were a half-dozen versions of the Crucifixion, plaster statues of Jesus and Mary, dusty crosses in wood and brass and nickel. And there was a ceramic cast of a saint's severed hand, which reached for the comfort of a bleeding heart embroidered on a satin cushion (p. 14).

In rebellion against this "panoply of religious objects" (p. 6), Angelo hangs his tie on the crucifix and makes "an obscene gesture at the collection of religious paraphernalia" (p. 9) as he leaves the house. But he leaves it only to confront more tarnished symbols of man's spiritual longing—a "shrewish virgin standing in a zinc tub" (p. 10) in a neighbor's yard, his cousin Frank compulsively fingering a St. Christopher medal, the Sacred Heart Hospital whose granite cross is covered with pigeon droppings, where plaster Madonnas lurk in every corridor and crucified Christs stare down on each bed. Despising the hypocrisy of such fetishes and talismen, Angelo comes near despising the anguished yearning which rests behind them. In his ruthless, calculated solitude, we can see the beginnings of that terrifying alienation which characterizes Berman and Nazerman. The sufferings he witnesses in the hospital only serve to drive him deeper into the brittle, protective shell:

And if he was brutalized by their constant assault, and if no pity was elicited in him, it was partly because he was in and out of there so often that the births and extinctions had no history. Besides, he knew the structure of the human body from his study; he held the vascular, skeletal, muscular drawings against his brain like a talisman against pain (p. 23).

In a similar gesture, Frank caresses his St. Christopher medal, and Angelo's mother stands before the kitchen window, "one hand toying with the silver cross that hung there" (p. 40).

VI *Apprenticeship*

Though linked by their superstitious faith in sacred totems, Angelo's two uncles (actually the brother and the cousin of his dead father) offer contrasting approaches to the religious experience, and since both might otherwise have played surrogate father roles, Angelo's rejection of them is significant in defining his precocious cynicism. Dominic represents the stern, authoritarian viewpoint which stresses the virtues of reverence and respect, but allows no room for simple gestures of human tenderness. Frank, on the other hand, knows the truth of compassion as well as the hard facts of the dehumanizing marketplace where he is exploited and must, in turn, exploit his young nephew. Wallant refers to Angelo as Frank's "true apprentice," and the fast-talking, miracle-cure-hunting uncle as his "shepherd." Wallant's father-son, master-apprentice theme becomes explicit when Frank muses, "You know how close I was with Dante, your old man. I mean we were more like brothers than cousins. . . . It's like you was my own son . . ." (p. 42). Frank more than once preaches the miracle of love and life to the troubled boy, thus foreshadowing Sammy's more telling lessons, but his message is too densely muffled by the wrappings of traditional Catholicism, too undermined by his own cynical mercantile philosophy to be acceptable to Angelo. Samuel Abel Cahan, on the other hand, first captures Angelo's attention by his disavowal of Christian mystery ["Tell me this: how did she have the baby if the husband didn't shtup her?" (p. 36)], but goes on to reveal to Angelo through a series of grotesque parables that the true mystery resides in man himself. He describes a singer he once heard whose voice was so beautiful that his listeners seemed paralyzed, unable to move. Then he tells of a butcher who cut his wife up in a refrigerator and kissed her all over when she was dead—"The funny thing was that he looked happier than anyone I ever saw" (p. 56). In contrast to this macabre tale, Sammy describes a fire in a Springfield orphanage and the heroic efforts of a fireman to rescue all the children, even though his own clothes are in flames. And when the last child is safe, the fireman mutters, "Well, that's all of 'em" (p. 56), and drops dead. A rich young man in Detroit one day sees an ugly, blind dwarf, reluctantly takes him by the arm to guide him, and spends the rest of his life leading this improbable companion. Angelo grows light-headed and uneasy as the Jewish orderly drones on and finally rushes from the room with a curse on his lips, but he moves out of the hospital into a night that seems "like a dream."

The oppressive heat that boils through the city only enhances this dream quality, further aggravating Angelo's own light-headedness. Reluctantly, he finds himself looking forward to the hospital encounters with Sammy, "sick with anticipation" (p. 60) as he makes his labyrinthine journeys through the wards and corridors of the hospital. When the peak of the heat comes, Angelo again sits listening to Sammy's "horrible and funny, sad and obscene" sermons. As the narrator begins, Angelo picks up a plum, bites it, and its sweet wetness is like a consecration. Sammy tells of an artist in a concentration camp commanded by an SS trooper to make a drawing from a photograph of the trooper's girl friend. Hopeful of an extra bread ration, the artist complies and then hides the drawing temporarily in a junction box. Later, another soldier comes to make repairs, opens the box, and immediately attacks the Jew for drawing a picture of his wife. When the Jew reveals the truth, he has two assailants, both "glaring bloody murder at him" (p. 63), and escapes only when the two SS men turn on each other. In contrast to this anecdote, Sammy recalls a fat, repulsive homoxexual with a passion for young boys who donates his eyes to restore the sight of a little girl, and a drug pusher named Irving Sterling who sits all night in the freezing rain, holding the hand of a prostitute trapped under a steel girder, and himself freezes to death. Wallant remarks that "the three listeners were like addicts" (p. 67). For every tale of cruelty or exploitation, Sammy spins two of bizarre dedication and love, and the effect of his "teachings" would be cloyingly sentimental if they did not finally merge into willful self-parody. The story of Irving Sterling's sterling death, with tears frozen on his face, merges with the later adventures of the prostitute whose hand he holds—a woman who despite her limp manages to continue a profitable career, with her young son as her pimp. "It was a real swell sight to see, I used to be really touched," Sammy remarks: "That kid would never, never let his mother work on Mother's day. . . (p. 68)." Angelo, struggling against the heat, the painful pressure he feels building inside himself, snarls, "What're you trying to prove?" (p. 68) What Sammy is trying to prove, of course, is man's capacity for suffering, for love, for redemption—above all, for the sweet mystery that is life, and which Angelo is not yet ready to accept. Significantly, Sammy has borne witness to each of these episodes; even the concentration-camp tale is about "my artist friend." And now Angelo, as disciple, must bear witness as well. He fights against Sammy's overture, and in his excitement faints; it is the first sure indication that, like Berman and Nazerman, he is being born again. As Angelo stumbles from the hospital, distant thunder brings the tantalizing promise of rain.

Angelo's ultimate defense against Sammy's teachings is to dismiss him as a drug pusher who uses the cover of his hospital job to turn a neat profit by injecting the pain-ridden patients. Yet he knows somehow that the simple facts of the case fail to explain Sammy, and when he learns that both the Jew and Howard Miller have been arrested for the attempted rape of Maria Alvarez, he feels "an onslaught of loneliness" (p. 85), "a massive crater in himself" (p. 85). The rain still has not come, and that night, unable to sleep, he goes into the yard, naked, to douse himself with the garden hose. Momentarily relieved, he imagines he can dismiss Sammy from his life, only to recognize that part of the wetness on his cheeks, "a warmer flow," comes from his own tears, that Sammy's apparent guilt gives him a "gnashing sensation of betrayal" (p. 87). Returning to the house, he discovers that his mother has watched his naked bathing, shocked by his lack of modesty, but more shocked by the suppressed passion that infuses her when Angelo's body reminds her of that of her own dead husband. She bemoans her drab, sere widowhood, and Angelo cynically advises her to sleep with her cross, still unable to give her understanding or compassion.

Later, when he sleeps, Angelo dreams "terrible, erotic dreams" involving "his mother and Theresa and Sammy and the girl with the tube in her throat" (p. 90). This, and the dreams that follow, are further testament to the painful, terrifying process of rebirth taking place inside the boy.

VII   *Bearing Witness*

Just as Sammy has borne witness in his tales of human terror and love, so must Angelo, in anticipation of his priestlike role, hear the tortured confession of the Russian orderly, Lebedov. Angelo has visited the hospital autopsy room to make a delivery, has been once more baffled by the detachment of the technician who works there—ironically, so much like the "scientific" objectivity Angelo has tried to embrace. As he leaves the morgue he wanders through a Dantesque collection of antiquated hospital machines that has "the look of an old dungeon strewn with elaborate instruments of torture, things that made people live in pain for a longer time than was good for them" (p. 102). And here he confronts Lebedov's pain, in the form of an anguished recitation of his life story:

"People is animal. What they are! I come from Russia. See my father drunk all time like crazy. Why? From being poor? From being scare? Maybe from being out in the sun, under sky like ant? Maybe from God, or from no God? Maybe from being hungry, from being alone in his head? Like a animal, but only worse, because something make him think he's not no animal? But what? My father. . . . He come home in the night, burn like fire. I feel him hot from outside already. I hear him bark like a wolf. . . . Mother, she close her eyes without cry. We all stop breathe. He come in twenty feet tall. He walk to Mother and pull back her head by her hair and look in her face with eyes all blood, and mouth open like to eat her. And he scream, 'You ugly, you so ugly! What I'm gonna do with you?' And then when she stay with her eyes closed like dead, he punch her face and her body, and when she fall down kick her all over. . . .

"He try to fuck my sister. Everybody screaming. Candle get knock over. Is dark like the bottom of the ocean we all rolling around together there. Finally candle get light again. . . . And Father is laying on the floor with Mother standing over him. Is knife in her hand and Father bleeding all over his chest. . . .

"People kill like anything. Nobody give a shit. What is there? I go in church when I'm a boy. I like the pretty color windows, clothes on priest, nice funny smell. I pray Jesus Chris' in white robe with hands on head of kids. So, so . . . don't make no goddam difference. *People!* Just only they drink, eat, grab things, take womans" (pp. 103–4).

For a time, a Marxist pamphlet seems to show Lebedov an alternative to this life, but in the end he becomes tired of the way "Still everybody smash one each other, same crazy stuff!" (p. 105). And so he too begins to "grab" things. In a passage strongly reminiscent of Steinbeck's *Of Mice and Men*, he describes his rapture for butterflies, and his horror at the way his father would capture them for him and reveal them crushed to a paste in his hand. Lebedov also crushes the beauty he tries to seize, as he has bruised and violated the body of Maria Alvarez. His oblique, stuttering confession concludes in an attempt at prayer which turns to agonized animal wailing.

Through Lebedov's confession, Sammy is freed, and Angelo is thus put in the role of his redeemer. He muses on "the ferocity of his quest for truth," finds himself opening up to his uncle Frank, spies on patients and on Sammy's antics in the children's ward, and begins to show a variety of unaccustomed, unpredictable responses. When he tries to recite the biological catechism which has defended him from the pain of feeling, he can think of the heart only as "a red valentine." Bewildered by the changes that seem to be happening inside him, he sits and listens to Sammy's description of his prison experiences—a passage much like that from *View of a Marvelous City*, quoted above, in Sammy's identification with the murderer. But the revelation that has come to Sammy extends the earlier message, for he has taken comfort and joy from his suffering. "It's so lonely not to suffer, so *lonely*. Who would want it if they knew? I don't say I *like* to suffer or *not* like to suffer. But *not* to!" (p. 120) When he professes not to understand the full meaning of the experience, Angelo accuses him of playing games: "Your angles have angles"; and Sammy replies, "And how do you know so much, *boychik*? . . . How do you know, for instance, that there's no such thing as magicians?" Angry and derisive, Angelo nonetheless comes perilously near the truth when he rejoins, "Maybe I ident-tiffied you with my father, Dr. Freud" (p. 121). Undaunted, Sammy offers a sacramental Last Supper: "A few cookies, some grape juice" (p. 123), and when Angelo has eaten and drunk, "it was as though something had been removed from him and something else put in its place" (p. 123).

Testing his disciple, Sammy makes him confront, through a peep-hole, the tender communications of a dying old man and his wife; he preaches that "you gotta love so much that you go insane or else turn cold like a machine" (p. 128); and to Angelo's angry cry, "Whatta you want to do? . . . Make the whole fucken world over?" he replies "Yeah. Yeah, *boychik*, that's what I had in mind" (p. 129). In the last of his stories—that of his own life, perhaps apocryphal—Sammy documents the apprenticeship that makes his picaresque sainthood possible. Growing up in a dank basement in New York, the son of a ragman, he had known a travesty of poverty but a wealth of love. His parents, "too stupid to be saints," nonetheless "breathed on me and touched me like I was Braille—we didn't know from love" (p. 133). When the ragman's pushcart is burned by Halloween pranksters, the father kisses his son good-bye and throws himself in front of a train. Thus, like Angelo, Sammy is orphaned, and as Angelo listens to this story, the rain falls outside and he himself has "a sensation of falling, disastrously" (p. 133).

When, the following day, Angelo finds Sammy lying on the sidewalk, moaning from the beating he has taken from people angered by the petition he has drawn up for Lebedov's forgiveness, he helps the orderly back to his rooming house. The dented mailboxes and jammed bells in the foyer anticipate the tenements managed by Norman Moonbloom, where devices of communication are also smashed and useless; the only communication here is in the obscene words and crude pornographic drawings that ornament the walls. But Sammy's room is different—an astonishing collage of magazine and newspaper pictures of people, of men, women, and children, the young and the old, violent and peaceful, rich and poor; it is a tableau of the "*kinder*" in whose name Sammy will plead for love. It is also a reminder of that community of man from which Angelo has willfully estranged himself. Fighting the "profound hurt" that pulses through his body, Angelo leaves to pen the Judaslike note that betrays Sammy to the hospital authorities.

In the final interview between the two orphans, Sammy imitates Angelo's own rationalist philosophy, rolling his eyes disinterestedly as he lectures a ward full of suffering patients, "I tell them, 'Look, it's all an accident—you know, with heredity and all.' I tell them, 'You got organs and they get beat up one way or another. I mean, there's answers for all of it,' I say to them" (p. 157). He recites clichés for them ["A woman may work from sun to sun, but a man's work is never done" (p. 158)], and then, rejecting both the role of cynical scientist and that of sideshow barker, he reveals the real Sammy to them: "We'll hang a bedpan on the wall, and you'll remember me, you'll remember me, you'll look forward to the next time I come around. Because I love you all, you hear? Nothing turns *my* stomach. I'll kiss your gallstones, your ulcers, your cancers, your bleeding piles—and they'll all disappear! It's all psychosomatic anyhow and I'm the miracle man" (p. 158). As miracle man, magician, savior, teacher, father, brother, dervish, clown, Sammy goes to his martyrdom. Exposed for his drug thefts, he hides in the gloomy cellar of the hospital, and Angelo sits vigil throughout the night, feeling *"sick, sick as hell . . ."* (p. 164). Once during the night the ubiquitous Sammy takes over the hospital's speaker system to recite the opening of the Kaddish: " 'Now hear this, now hear this. . . .' A muffled cry from someone was followed by frantic calls too far away from the microphone to make out; and then, clear and unhurried, in Sammy's high, clinging voice, *'Yis-gad-dal v'yis-kad-dash sh'meh rab-bo . . .'* " (p. 166). Once again, in summoning up the prayer of mourning, Wallant stresses the idea of brotherhood, the celebration of life's seemingly infinite progressions. Sammy makes a far more eloquent appeal to Angelo's buried resources for love and regeneration than Sister Louise with her tight-mouthed recitation of the wonders of Christ's love.

The following morning a radio blares the saccharine organ theme of a radio soap opera, a parody of love, when Sammy appears to beg the parents of the dead Maria Alvarez to forgive Lebedov. Dressed in white, his arms widespread, he preaches his ultimate sermon: "Love one another, love me, love you. . . ." He shouts for joy, "It's here and now! . . . You can touch me and I can touch you. It won't be any better. Love me, O *kinder*" (pp. 171-72). The bereaved father's single, faint touch, a gesture of disgust and confusion, sends Sammy sailing with "fluid grace" through the air, to be immolated on the iron spikes of a fence. As Angelo looks into his dying eyes, he knows that this is Sammy's final joke, and he begins to laugh, thinking, "How it hurt now—straight up through his guts to his heart" (p. 174).

VIII   *From the Desert to the Garden*

In the weeks that follow Sammy's death, Angelo, "like some desert dweller" (p. 177), withdraws catatonically from the world to make his last and most trying vigil, from which he emerges to comfort his lonely, afflicted sister.then he learns of the insurance money, the symbolic legacy that Sammy has left him; and for the first time since the orderly's death, he is able to weep—perplexed tears that signal his awakening from the deep, dark sleep that was his old life. For a time, he returns to the rituals of his former existence, but with the coming of spring, when "the trees were new again," he uses the insurance money to leave the scene of his suffering. The shrewish neighborhood Madonna still stands in her zinc tub, and the familiar concrete cross dominates the old hospital that will soon be razed in the name of progress. Angelo seems to hear "the dim burble of children's laughter" and a voice whispering the word *"boychik,"* and he gropes for understanding of all that he has now witnessed, of the lessons he has learned from the Jewish clown:

And a blade twitched into his heart, beginning that slow, massive bleeding he would never be able to stop, no matter what else he might accomplish. He was surprised and puzzled as he walked with that mortal wound in him, for it occurred to him that, although the wound would be the death of him, it would be the life of him too (p. 184).

Just as Sol Nazerman's capacity for rebirth was foreshadowed in the tenderness he showed his harassed nephew, so in *The Children at the Gate* Angelo DeMarco's true spiritual capacity is revealed by the tenderness he shows his retarded sister, Theresa. In some respects her numb, incommunicative existence is a shadow of Angelo's own: "aimlessness was the shape of her life" (p. 4). And Theresa symbolizes in the novel all the abused, lonely children who cry at the gate for comfort. Once, when neighborhood boys screamed insults at Theresa, a younger Angelo had thrown himself on them in full fury, "calm and determined and clearly intent on total destruction" (p. 8), but afterwards he returns to Theresa "with that same terrifying calm" (p. 8). It is Angelo who encourages the girl to eat, combs her long hair, and teaches her, in one of the novel's most lyric and harmonious moments, to operate a simple loom.

Watching her children from the window, one hand toying with her silver cross, Esther DeMarco can almost recapture the old romantic dream of a close, protective family. But Esther, significantly, remains obscure behind the glass, whereas "Angelo was clear and fine as he knelt devoutly, the colors of the stained-glass light covering him with a look of love and gentleness" (p. 40).

The promise of that tenderness Angelo shows the perpetual child who is his sister stands out the more dramatically since the abuse of children figures so frequently in Wallant's novel. The pavilion of the Sacred Heart Hospital, which contains the children's ward, is more often the scene of the action than the wards and private rooms that house adults, and it is there—before children whose bodies are wracked by pain, deformed, burned, implanted with prosthetic devices—that Sammy Cahan delivers some of his most memorable performances. Sammy's own parables contain several examples of love and sacrifice in the name of the innocent young—a pervert who donates his eyes to a young blind girl, a fireman who dies rescuing children from an orphanage, a child-sized dwarf who finds someone to guide him. Such moments contrast starkly with Lebedov's attempted rape of Maria Alvarez and with the anguished recollection of his father's rape of his sister. And Sammy recalls similar horrors from his own tenement childhood: "Up on the fourth floor there was a skinny house painter. It came out he was screwing his daughter. I know he was the saddest creatuue I ever saw—used to cry all the time, drunk or sober" (p. 131). Similarly, he remembers the butcher's wife: "Her kid one time was acting up in some way she didn't like, and she shoved the kid into the refrigerator for a while" (p. 131). Such grotesque anecdotes recall the Grand Inquisitor episode of *The Brothers Karamazov*, in which the senseless suffering of a child is used as a challenge to the existence (or at least the beneficence) of God, or the agonizing death of the child in Albert Camus's *La Peste*, where the incident so horribly underscores the absurdity of the plague-ridden world. But in Wallant's work, as in Dostoevsky's and Camus's, a few men will be able to rise above these negative proofs, to spin values from their own spirits—or to derive them from the absurd struggle itself.

Angelo's apprenticeship to the wandering Jew, Samuel Abel Cahan, belongs to one of the most resilient traditions in

American literature. Often, in our most classic novels, a young hero finds spiritual companionship and kinship with another, often older, man. As a beardless youth, Natty Bumppo is initiated into the mysteries of woodslore by the noble Mohican, Chingachgook; but the initiation brings more than physical skills, for it instills a reverence for nature, a sense of harmony with creation, of respect for honest, manly conduct, and distrust of the motives of polite civilization. Melville's Ishmael finds his Queequeg, and at a critical moment in his life, when, as he reports in lines that might well apply to Angelo, he feels himself "growing grim about the mouth; whenever it is a damp, drizzly November in my soul; whenever I find myself involuntarily pausing before coffin warehouses, and bringing up the rear of every funeral I meet."

Huckleberry Finn finds surrogate father, companion, and teacher in the runaway slave, Jim; Saul Bellow's Henderson apprentices himself to King Dahfu; and Faulkner's Ike McCaslin is lovingly molded to maturity by the Indian Sam Fathers. Of all these novels about young spiritual apprentices and their wise, often enigmatic masters, the one most closely parallel to Wallant's is Ken Kesey's *One Flew Over the Cuckoo's Nest,* a book published the year of Wallant's death. Though the hospital setting in Kesey's novel is far more distorted, more sinister, one again encounters the image of a world in which the spirit of man is of less worth than his flesh, and both Sister Louise and Big Nurse are crisply, deadeningly efficient administrators. Into these static environments burst two of the most original comic characters in contemporary literature—Sammy Cahan and Randle McMurphy, who foment revolution in their very exuberance for life. Kesey's description of McMurphy immediately establishes his cousinage with Sammy:

The way he talks, his wink, his loud talk, his swagger all remind me of a car salesman or a stock auctioneer—or one of those pitchmen you see on a sideshow stage, out in front of his flapping banners, standing there in a striped shirt with yellow buttons, drawing the faces off the sawdust like a magnet.[3]

McMurphy's comic antics and his eventual martyrdom (surrounded, like Sammy's, by allusions to the death of Christ) are witnessed by Chief Broom, an Indian who has sealed himself off from the world, but whose apathy is steadily eroded by McMurphy's infectious embrace of life. And through the new strength he acquires from these lessons, Chief Broom escapes two prisons—that of the hospital, and the more terrifying prison of the self. Kesey's novel reverses the traditional pattern in which a naive white boy sits at the feet of a man of darker race, with the clear cultural implication that more "primitive," basic men, men closer to the rhythms of the natural world, can reteach lessons which a prolapsed Western society has long forgotten. In *One Flew Over the Cuckoo's Nest,* however, it is the Indian, the ur-American, who is transformed and thus restored to his tribe and his heritage. Wallant's work follows the more classic pattern. Jesus Ortiz is a black, though he may well have some mixture of Puerto Rican blood, and despite his recitation of ancestry, Sammy's origins remain obscure. When Angelo asks him where he comes from, the Jew replies, "Oh, all over" (p. 35). But whatever their individual configurations, all these relationships between men remain initiatory, ceremonial, sacred, and all conclude by teaching a lonely, estranged "orphan" the essential lessons of community, commitment, and love.

Despite the particular affection he felt for *The Children at the Gate,* Wallant came near abandoning it on several occasions. Harcourt, Brace rejected the first version, *View of a Marvelous City,* and Wallant almost immediately began rewriting the novel, but he often found the project burdensome and later remarked to his editor, Dan Wickenden, that it was the hardest work he had ever done. His wife, Joyce, insisted he return to the manuscript and repeatedly urged him on, encouraged him to read troublesome sections aloud and declared it her favorite of all his writings. The book was, appropriately, dedicated to her. Before he left for Europe in 1962, Wallant submitted a completely reworked manuscript to Harcourt, Brace, but because of his haste to deliver it, the novel never received the kind of final polishing which the author had given his previous published works. He continued to revise *The Children at the Gate* and *The Tenants of Moonbloom* during his European travels, but only the latter was completed to his satisfaction. The task of preparing *The Children at the Gate* for publication was undertaken after Wallant's death by Dan Wickenden, and a study of his editorial changes reveals the highest literary integrity and an uncompromising devotion to Wallant's intentions. Most of Wickenden's revisions involve paring away the occasional excessive word or phrase—for Wallant never entirely escaped his tendency toward lyrical inflation—regularizing punctuation, tightening sentence structures, and correcting inconsistencies with respect to physical details of the story.[4] It is still Wallant's voice that we hear, in the early stages of its transformation to a new comic vigor; yet one can only regret that the author was unable to see this most troublesome, most beloved of his writings through the final stages of revision and refinement.

CHAPTER 7

The Tenants of Moonbloom

I *The Moonbloom Notebook*

IN the autumn of 1961, as he anxiously awaited the decision on his Guggenheim application, Edward Lewis Wallant underwent a significant metamorphosis in the view of his role as an artist—one that was to result in the astonishingly mature achievements of the last fourteen months of his life. Only two years before, he had added the following note to a personnel form: "I am married, father of three children. In my spare time I paint and do some writing (managing to sell a few short stories in the process)." No longer could he blithely describe writing as a "spare-time" activity, for he had an increasingly vital, increasingly urgent sense that this was his ultimate vocation. Once content to work at the narrow kitchen table in the small house he and his family occupied in Norwalk, he now chafed about the domestic interruptions and professional distractions that prevented him from dedicating himself to his craft with complete intensity. At this critical moment in his life, he began to keep a diary. On the endpapers at the front of the leather-spined ledger, he described his children playing on a lawn "littered with brown leaves," and yearned to accept the commonplace happiness of family, social accommodation, modest business success, but that conventional role was now staunchly opposed by the vague, phantomlike shape of that "fertility" which could only be expressed in his writing.

On October 2, 1961, the first dated entry in the journal, he sits watching a small steel ball that rolls along a track to power a clock, and sees in it an image of his own frustration: "—as though time didn't get anywhere really—just moved back and forth in a small chamber." He reads a biography of Thomas Wolfe, watches a television documentary on Ernest Hemingway, and thinks of "how little I live as a writer—how little miserable time I have to work." Yet worse, he feels that "what I've done so far, what I'm doing now isn't nearly big enough," and yearns for the freedom to explore themes of "life, death, love, responsibility, mystery, God, lust, fear, guilt, compassion, beauty" of which his earlier work has shown only shadows. Later in the day, the children asleep and the house resonant with the ticking of the clock, his wife's bathwater running, the discipline of the craftsman returns: "Try to settle down. Finish that thing with Angelo and Sammy—for now just this draft." The entry for October 2 concludes with more dreams of Europe, a break from routine: "I'll never do real great things this way." And then, at the foot of the page, occurs the first germ of the narrative that would be entitled *The Tenants of Moonbloom:* "Gimple (different story) man named Norman (pale with dark blue beard) 'You "nuyyed" me'—Gimple and Norman."

Two weeks later, Norman's story would begin to unfold in this same journal with dazzlingly virtuoso ease, for Wallant by then had found the writer's retreat he sought. On October 4, 1961, he looked for a room in New York where he could devote occasional week nights to his writing. Wandering the city, he assembled images of its inhabitants, all "pursuing dim little grails" and "seizing hazy ecstasies." He envisioned women seeking "for love or love or love," men leaving them "soiled and humiliated," and "the lonely, savage fatherless sons fighting all the big men—the mother's lovers." Then, in a passage that directly foreshadows *The Tenants of Moonbloom,* he writes of

The old skinny supers who live in rough-walled *gratis* rooms and mumble as they reach toward the panel of keys—"Let's see now, 5-A, 5-A," and there are always big, full-color nudes stuck on their walls,— great rosy, full breasted girls who could crush all the skinny supers. But they must pretend otherwise—they must be great dream ravishers as they sit in their gratis rooms listening to all the illicit bed squealings of their furnished rooms.

Wallant himself had seen such men during his day of searching for a room in which he could work, and they had nudged his imagination as surely as the old refugee whose pawnshop he had once visited. It was proof—if proof were needed—of the wisdom of his search. Meanwhile, he confessed that "partly I know it's the *idea* of being a 'real' writer—solitude and that nonsense. I admit my affectations but some of it is real—my desire to write the best I can. I'll try it for a while."

The following night, October 5, he sits in his new room listening to the sounds of the city, watching the view from his window: "taxis, trucks pummeling the street—a man carrying his shaving kit down 53rd Street so blithely as though N. Y. were one big Y.M.C.A. and him on the way to the john." The characters who will populate Norman Moonbloom's shabby apartment house seem to enter the very room in which Wallant sits writing: he makes notes about an old, ugly commercial artist who airbrushes figures of nude models, of an aspiring young artist who yearns to create works of genuine, lasting beauty, of a "truly courageous man," a "great Comic creature but *not* a fool."

On October 17 Wallant spends the third night in his furnished room in the city, and notes that the revisions of *The Children at the Gate* are almost completed. Earlier in the evening he had once more wandered the city streets, and once more the sense is one of Moonbloom's drama taking shape from the stones and the flesh of the city:

I spent an evening wandering from Mott St. and a mouldering, dark hole with soft bulging walls & ancient toilet stopped up with filth—to East 53rd and Fifth with its posh bars and curried people all displayed in special lights—like a weird fair—one end of the earth to the other— Babylon—The whole world is Babylon—but—the paradox is—there are millions upon millions of redeemers never able to get untracked. Sufferers—Oh I love and pity—make it work, how to make it work?
    To work on my new novel.

At this point, the dated diary entries stop, and the single word "Random" appears—no doubt to indicate that Wallant now intends to set down some of his scattered thoughts about the novel that is so persistently shaping itself in his imagination. Tentatively, he entitles it (and the title is heavily underscored in the journal) *The Man of Responsibility.* He continues to think of Gimple, the erotic, exuberant Jewish clown, as a figure in the work, though not its hero. Indeed, the first problem Wallant envisions is how to make his man of responsibility seem sufficiently heroic "(beside, for example, Gimple)." After this single, parenthetic expression of doubt, a scenario for the novel begins to flow with what was, to judge by the handwriting, astonishing speed:

Man a rent-collector.

A landlord who inherits property and who wanted to be something else. Brother very happy with the money and power—he is oppressed by it. He is 34—brother is 52—for years a wanderer—comes to visit on his way someplace else—Gimple (brother-father)—or agent for houses—owned by his two brothers—salaried—in charge of rent collection. His involvement with the tenants, the growing worry and sense of responsibility.

The very punctuation of this passage, the first Moonbloom entry, shows Wallant's groping for a clarifying conception of his hero. The dashes suggest, I think, more than the speed with which the passage was written, but the confusion that attends the conception so long as it pivots round the overpowering figure of Gimple. Happily, the old man would soon be dropped from the plot of the novel, and the number of brothers reduced to one, so that increasing focus could be centered on "the man of responsibility" himself. A few more somewhat hesitant passages follow, describing the way Norman's brothers had persuaded their wealthy grandfather that Norman was a scholar who should be sent to university while the real-estate empire should be left to them. When Wallant begins to mute the problem of Moonbloom's relationship to his behemoth father, the conception of the hero becomes remarkably sure, firmly detailed:

After much futile schooling—he had never been cut out for a scholar—"I'm just pale and shy and irritable"—everyone took it for some kind of moody genius. Now, after college and teaching for ten years in a small city—he has come back to work for the brothers, at a modest salary. He acts as agent & rent collector for their apartments while they concentrate on Industrial properties.

He becomes more and more obsessed by the tenants. He is harsh, exasperated, sometimes patiently bored, sometimes amused, sometimes aroused sensually. But at night he cannot sleep and he feels the world crowding his brain. He reads the papers, listens to the radio—pities himself, scorns himself.

A relationship with a woman finally and irrevocably commits the rent-collector to all the plaints of the tenants; this near-sentimental motivation for the hero's transformation happily becomes only a minor chord in the final orchestration of the novel. In this early sketch, the ubiquitous Gimple pays a visit "on his way to somewhere else," and attempts to take Norman away with him, but his youngest son is determined to pursue what he calls his *"career,"* and feels "a queer and melancholy power" in his decision.

II   A New Narrative Ease

Wallant had explored the father-son relationship in all the novels, both published and unpublished, as well as most of the short stories he had written before *The Tenants of Moonbloom*, and though he would return to the theme in the works he began shortly before his death, perhaps he felt he had temporarily exhausted its resources; even in *The Children at the Gate*, father-son metaphors are submerged beneath those of fraternity. And perhaps he also recognized that Gimple was too over-shadowing a figure to play off against the more delicate, tentative person of Norman Moonbloom; Gimple is a fairy-tale hero, while Norman is simply and triumphantly a man. At any event, in the final draft of the novel Gimple remains only in the dreamily remembered figure of the robust, wandering father who once brought the clean crispness of a snowy winter day into the life of his son. Equally strategic was Wallant's later decision to reduce the brothers to a single character who does not even appear in the novel save as a disembodied voice at the end of a telephone wire—an abstract representative of the values and mores of the marketplace. The story thus becomes exclusively Norman's, as Wallant realized when he noted, "The character of Norman must be most thought about," and he will assume at least the potential for Gimple's legendary zeal for life. Once Wallant has resolved this narrative complication, he can proceed with far greater assurance. He now entitles the novel *The Tenants* or *The City Dwellers*, and it takes even clearer shape in his mind:

Make it 4 weeks long. *Start with Norman* (on the job for a year?

already—and up till that day walking blindered and ear-plugged and clothespinned-nosed through the buildings filtering out all but a dim impression of the tenants that seethes in his brain in sleep, not clear enough to keep him up or even to be held, visible, in the unconscious light of dream.) Yet he must have been covered only with egg shell. One hard-pointed thing exposed him and he was like a man in deep water who has never tried to swim.
So it's Norman coming awake to them.

Wallant then describes the complaints, dreams, concerns with which the tenants besiege their rent-collector, the insistent telephone calls from his brothers, and how Norman gradually begins "to see the tenants with the odd sensation of clair-voyance."

There follows a kind of novelistic aside in which Wallant articulates the love theme that is central to all his work. The prose is embarrassingly self-indulgent—an example of the overwrought style the author could produce when he was being consciously "literary," but the passage nonetheless throws interesting light on Wallant's intentions:

Is love entirely something we learn? It is partly fear—a manifestation of our projecting ourselves into others and then feeling that precious bits of ourselves exist in other people. So we fear them, yearn for them, pity them as we naturally do for ourselves. And this ability to locate bits of our spirits in others is what makes us unique among animals.

And our dreams are another aspect of our tendency to "flake off" emotionally. Some of the flakes come to reside in other people but some seem to just float in vagrant breezes, to dance up and catch the light in ever-changing prismatic reflections—we dream—that is, we look forward or backward with a strange fascination. Always there exists an odd, illusory sensation of hope. . . . And sometimes we may even approach death possessed by that odd hope as though we feel that the motes of feeling will continue to exist even after the parent consciousness has ceased to live.

Scarcely a phrase in the passage suggests the unique narrative voice so abundantly apparent in both *The Tenants of Moonbloom* and the existing fragment of *Tannenbaum's Journey,* and the reader of Wallant's journal is left totally unprepared for the way in which the lines that follow crackle with life; after what almost certainly amounted to no more than a few days of jottings about the shape of this new work, Wallant was ready to begin. From the handwriting one suspects that he was not copying or working from notes but composing directly into the notebook, and doing so at top speed. The flow of the passage is superb, and in the three notebook pages covered by the following passage, there are only four corrections:

"On Thirteenth Street the house is falling apart." Norman was undramatic; a phone demanded no expression. "The roof leaks—the toilets back up. The stair bannister fell off and the furnace is broken. The old man on the top leaves food around and the place is filled with *la cucaracha*. There are no lights in the halls and there is a hole in the 3rd floor hallway six inches wide. Also some kids broke a pane in the front hall window."

"Broke a window!" His brother, Irwin, howled, making the delicate diaphragm reverberate in the phone receiver. "You got to be more alert, Norman."

"Alert," Norman said, smiling helplessly at his ten foot square office.

"Eddie and I depend on you. We can't be bothered with the details of those four houses. You know how busy we are with other things. Is it too much to ask of you to take care of everything? You are our kid brother. We trust you—we employ you. All you have to do is handle a few details of four small houses. Eddie and I deal in nothing less than 6 figures. Your responsibilities are paltry beside ours. How can you allow windows to get broken?"

"Tell me why you jumped at the windows? I told you the whole house. . . ."

"Some things are acts of God," Irwin admonished.

"Why not windows then?"

"Norman, I have no time to quarrel. Take care of all those things without bothering us. Where's your initiative?"

"Initiative I could maybe dig up. For the roof and the bannister and the plumbing and electricity, I need money."

"You have the complete freedom to draw on your corporation account."

"Blood from a stone. Irwin, it is empty, bare, depleted. There *is* no more in the account."

"Ohh, Norman!"

"And I owe Gaylord."

"Gaylord is an uppity Negro. He's lazy and not conscientious."

"Say what you will—he takes care of the four houses, however inadequately, for forty dollars a week."

"Norman, do you realize that mine and your brother Eddie's time is worth roughly fifty dollars an hour? I have wasted a good forty dollars already on this."

"On Mott Street the wall is swelling—it is going to collapse on Basellicci. In the 70th Street house the elevator did not pass inspection. On Second Avenue the ceilings are wet and the fireman said the wiring was so bad he wouldn't even take a bribe for it—said he drew the line at murder." Norman was tireless but Irwin was not.

"Goddam it Norman, you're a big disappointment is all I can say."

"The insurance grace period on 13th Street is almost up," Norman went on indefatigably.

"I'll put five hundred in the checking account this noon! Now don't let me hear from you for a long time."

The click couldn't express the power of his brother's violent hanging up but Norman could visualize it. He put his phone down with great delicacy and smiled palely at the dusty afternoon sunlight.

A comparison of this early, hastily written version of Norman's first conversation with Irwin and the scene that opens the novel itself shows how firm and pointed Wallant's conception of the work had become, how effortlessly the novel was now being written. Indeed, if *The Children at the Gate* was the most difficult book Wallant had composed, *The Tenants of Moonbloom* was the easiest. Other than the deletion of a second brother, the final version of the conversation quoted above chiefly demonstrates an intensification of the comic voice which Wallant was trying with growing assurance. Thus, the simple statement that "on Thirteenth Street the house is falling apart" becomes "on Thirteenth Street . . . the roof leaks so badly that the rats are leaving the building" (p. 4). When the news of a broken window provokes Irwin to demand his younger brother be more alert, Wallant follows his command with the following line:

"Alert," Norman said, smiling helplessly at his ten foot square office.

In the novel, the line reads

"Alert," Norman said, smiling helplessly at his grotto (p. 4).

When Irwin admonishes Norman by reminding him of the "much more complicated transactions" in which he is involved, Wallant observes that "he was so reasonable that Norman was tempted to kiss the mouthpiece" (p. 5). Such revisions and retouchings of the original passage sharpen our sense of Norman Moonbloom as "moon-calf," as the sweet-tempered, ineffectual *schlemiel* who differs so radically from Wallant's other isolated heroes—from the grieving, raging Berman, the rambunctious Gimple, the tormented Nazerman, the cynical Angelo and wisecracking Sammy. That sense is extended in the alterations Wallant made to the lines describing the conclusion of the conversation between the two brothers. The first version reads:

The click couldn't express the power of his brother's violent hanging up but Norman could visualize it. He put his phone down with great delicacy and smiled palely at the dusty afternoon sunlight.

In the revised, expanded version:

The tiny click in the receiver couldn't begin to suggest the force with which Irwin must have slammed down the phone. Norman felt a certain sense of nobility in putting *his* phone back on the cradle with exquisite delicacy. Then he had to smile wanly at the dusty, secondhand sunlight and the misspelled obscenities chalked in the well his office rested in (p. 7).

In revising his earlier work, Wallant often sought to highlight his intentions by overlaying his prose with a self-conscious poetic language, freighted ponderously with metaphor. Here the revisions are far more craftsmanlike, more disciplined, and they provide eloquent testimony both to the novelist's heightened sense of vocation and to the shaping force of his fictional conception.

In later versions of the novel the father figure once more rather aggressively intrudes, and for a time Norman is pictured as a fatherless, brotherless young man (with a background vaguely like Wallant's own) who is employed by two cousins. Ultimately, Wallant would return to a picture of the hero strikingly like that worked out in the notebook. Since he usually composed directly on the typewriter, this holograph manuscript of a novel is virtually unique, though a few handwritten pages of *Tannenbaum's Journey* were also found among Wallant's papers after his death. The new Olivetti he had bought, however, was at home in Norwalk, where he continued to work on the final draft of *The Children at the Gate,* and the urgency and excitement with which Norman's story unfolded for him demanded immediate

expression. The notations for *The Tenants of Moonbloom,*
beginning with the simple phrase "Man named Norman," cover
more than 100 hand-written pages, concluding with a poignant
description of Norman's birth to involvement and pain:

> He was a Romantic without portfolio. Unsureness made his relation-
> ship with women fall wide of any mark. He blundered toward love,
> blindfolded, and pinned the donkey tail where the ear should have
> been. His sexual experiences had been stumblings into orgasm and had
> always left him bewildered—the women had expected too little or he
> had expected too much.
> Conventionally he was a failure—his brothers could have told you so.
> Still, he had this dream—whatever it was—and he had courage and
> humor—it would take a lot to extinguish him he knew with modest
> certainty.

HIS BIRTH TO PAIN
AND INVOLVEMENT

Coming when he is working on Basellecci's wall and it bursts in a
broken pipe full of shit and water.

III   *The Man of Responsibility*

Various loose sheets of paper are tucked into the Moonbloom
notebook, which from their contents would seem to date from
the same period in which Wallant created the earliest version of
his last completed work. The pages contain both direct and
indirect allusions to the tragicomic rent-collector, "a man
besieged by love and pity and frustration." In a passage which
recalls the original title of the novel, *The Man of Responsibility,*
Wallant writes,

> My theme would be *responsibility:* to others, to one's self. I wish to
> explore the strange conflict of interests with which most men are
> assailed, almost from birth to death; those obligations thrust upon us by
> society, religion, and even more inexplicably by the peculiar and
> unidentifiable organ we call our emotions, our psyche, our "hearts," our
> souls.

Wallant's rent-collector, Norman Moonbloom, is initially deaf to
the cries of the heart, but—unlike Wallant's earlier heroes—not
because of any trauma which has blunted his emotional life.
Moonbloom has withdrawn from the world through sheer

inanition, content to be a passive collector rather than inceptor; his emotional hibernation, his anomie, is not the result of victimization by fate, but a survival mechanism which for a time, at least, shields him from the pain of the tortured urban landscape through which he must move. Like Nathanael West's Miss Lonelyhearts, who struggles to maintain his detachment from the tormented advice-seekers who share with him their crippled dreams, Norman Moonbloom will suddenly find the cultivated shell of detachment pierced by the cries of his communicants. When this occurs, both men undergo symbolic periods of fever and sickness from which they will emerge with a sense of messianic mission. As Miss Lonelyhearts explains the process,

He too considers the job a joke, but after several months at it, the joke begins to escape him. He sees that the majority of the letters are profoundly humble pleas for moral and spiritual advice, that they are inarticulate expressions of genuine suffering. He also discovers that his correspondents take him seriously. For the first time in his life he is forced to examine the values by which he lives. This examination shows him that he is the victim of the joke and not its perpetrator.[1]

Similarly, his encounters with the tenants compel Moonbloom to "examine the values by which he lives," and in doing so he realizes far sooner than Wallant's other heroes, and with far less emotional chaos, the expediency of radical commitment and action.

Norman Moonbloom is in his thirty-third year when the novel opens. After spending fourteen years as a student, wandering among majors in podiatry, accounting, art, literature, dentistry, and the rabbinate, he settles in lower Manhattan to manage four apartment houses owned by his brother Irving. Other than the immense fedora hat which makes him "look like a child imitating a gangster" (p.9), he possesses none of the outward, superficial mannerisms of rebel or clown. It is, in fact, his very commonplace manner and appearance that lend special poignancy to his eventual transfiguration. As the novel opens, Moonbloom is still successful in playing his escapist role. His "underground" existence is suggested by the office in which he works, set below the level of the street, so that when he gazes through the window he sees only "people's bodiless heads." In this fetal retreat, with

"fleshy pink" walls, he exists "between daydream and nothing."
The sunlight that enters the office must "bend to get down
there," so that here he is literally shut away from life. Wallant's
choice of imagery repeatedly reinforces this view of the hero:

He walked lightly and his face showed no awareness of all the
thousands of people around him because he traveled in an eggshell
through which came only subdued light and muffled sound (p. 9).

The life in the building moved dimly around him like the pulsing
movement perceived through new ice (p. 10).

He stepped into his own apartment, and his deep, relieving sigh was
that of a man to whom hermitage is an ever-present temptation (p. 30).

When he washed the pot and the dish, he had an image of himself,
thin, dark, idiotically placid, sealed into a hermetic globe whose
thinness gave him only the flickering colors of the outside (p. 32).

Unlike Wallant's earliest chronicles of the hero's progress
along the thorny existential path of "becoming," in *The Tenants
of Moonbloom* the hero's transformation is not the culmination of
some prolonged and terror-ridden dark night of the soul, but
seems imminent from the first chapter of the novel. Even as
Norman sits listening to Irwin's persistent "rannana rannana," he
thinks of himself as a hall of mirrors: "within him his dream was
an infinite series of reflections and all he could be sure of was
that it existed and made him sure that *he* existed" (p. 4).
Wallant's earlier characters have abandoned their dreams and
must rediscover them, while it is only necessary for Moonbloom
to refine his and to seek their articulation, understanding that at
the very moment vital contact with the world is made possible,
there will be tremendous pain: "It was like the fear of death; he
could ignore it most of the time, although it was implacably
there, to touch him with the very tip of its claw in moments of
frustration . . ." (p. 8). Meanwhile, for as long as he is able, the
rent-collector seeks to sustain the cultivated veneer of detachment. He makes the weekly rounds of the decaying apartment
houses, collecting rents, filling out phony receipts, evasively
promising repairs to faulty wiring, dripping sinks, condemned
elevators and malfunctioning appliances. His forty-six tenants
form a microcosm of the city's outcasts and rejects, hustlers and
hipsters, dreamers and dream-destroyers.

As Norman makes his rounds, he yearns for freedom, for the insulated, womblike life of his own apartment, but the tenants persistently infiltrate his consciousness. The Lublins, former concentration-camp inmates, complain of a dripping faucet; the Spragues, a young married couple, contemplate the wife's swelling pregnancy with bewilderment and faint surprise; an elderly Italian schoolteacher, Basellecci, offers Moonbloom the mead of his fresh-brewed coffee, and rages against the bulging toilet wall that he indicts as the source of his prolonged constipation; Sheryl Beeler dotes on her retired pharmacist father, who can only see his blowsy, promiscuous daughter in the Shirley Temple role he created for her as a girl; Kram, a hunchback who retouches pictures for magazines, has abandoned all desire: he has no complaints for the rent collector. One is again reminded of the gallery of grotesques Nathanael West created in both *Miss Lonelyhearts* and *The Day of the Locust*, and as Moonbloom moves through the rent-collecting cycle— from the "best" apartment building on Second Avenue to the "worst" on Thirteenth Street—the analogy is only strengthened. Moonbloom visits Wade Johnson, an embittered schoolteacher who takes out his frustrations and his intellectual pretensions on an adoring son; an aging ingénue with hyperthyroid eyes who seeks in a string of lovers a father for her child; an old, tubercular Jew whose identity is established only by his coughing, and whose wife struggles to gild their poverty with gentility; a former concentration-camp attendant, Ilse Moeller, who thrives on her hatred for the Jews; Karloff, an ancient Russian Jew who lives in indescribable filth; Sugarman, the candy-butcher who survives only by his incessant clowning; a black homosexual novelist with a heritage of hatred and oppression; a boxer who studies acting and whose compulsive cleanliness is a defense against memories of a sordid childhood; and finally, "Louie, a Jewish gnome," who lives in cramped quarters under the roof and dreams of visits to his sister on Long Island, who welcomes him only as an occasional baby-sitter.

As Moonbloom leaves Louie's apartment, the weekly round of rent-collecting complete, he feels that "the distance between him and the nearest passer-by was infinite" (p. 69); in the brisk winter air he muses "on the possibility of thermostatically controlled clothing that would keep one's body at a constant temperature" (p. 69), but such a womblike existence is not to be his destiny. Distracted, he fails to see a drunk vomit on the sidewalk, but some of it splashes on him, and later, at home, he sees "an unexplained stain on his pant leg" (p. 70). He has been "marked" by the world from which he sought to be isolated. Moonbloom has already felt somewhat ill; he now enters a period of sickness much like Angelo's, or the feverish collapse that precedes Miss Lonelyhearts' religious experience. Briefly, a plumbing problem in the house on Thirteenth Street takes him away from his sickbed, and in a scene reminiscent of *The Human Season* he watches Bodien, the unfrocked plumber, fumble among "the dust-furred pipes" in the dank cellar, feeling all the while "the threat of permanent eviction." In a parody of *The Waste Land*, "gunk" is removed from the pipes, and water once more flows to the tenants' apartments. Moonbloom returns to his sickbed, seeking release in a daydream, only to find that the dream

. . . was occupied, filled like a vast hall with all the tenants. Katz tootled his trumpet in greeting, and a gelatinous note fell *splat* on the ballroom floor. Basellecci aimed a wide-mouthed cannon at him and smiled with his canonical face. Two people were screaming. He was screaming, and he woke up filled with embarrassment and fear and lying in a drenching sweat (pp. 76–77).

IV   *Breaking the Spirit's Sleep*

In the five critical days that follow, Moonbloom reaches back into the past, unconsciously seeking—like Berman and Nazerman—the base from which he can build a new relationship to the world. There is no recognizable pattern to the parade of memories with which the rent-collector is visited, though all of them are touched by a feeling of "virginal terror." He recalls himself at the age of four, making discord on a piano keyboard while his grandmother hums "Melancholy Baby" in the background; at twelve, using split peas as soldiers in a game or war; at ten, wrapped in "fairy-tale ease," his grandmother behind him, listening to radio reports of European horrors; at fourteen, being insulted by the boy with whom he competes for a pretty girl's attention; at three, eating ice cream, feeling his grandmother's tears, being wrapped "in something light and soft and very strong. In the morning he will find it has become his skin" (p. 80). Throughout these memories, the protecting, nurturing figure of the grandmother constantly reappears, a steady female presence that insulates the boy from pain and hence is the primal source of his later, near-catatonic withdrawal from life. At eighteen he leaves for college, but sitting at his desk "he expects momentarily to hear his grandmother humming" (p. 80). At an indeterminate age he sits in the dust, building walls and prisons for scurrying ants while "far over the fences he hears Irwin in a ball game" (p. 80). This older brother has always been the active, aggressive one; it is he who is destined for the empty success of the real-estate hustler, while Norman remains pampered and withdrawn. In another dream he recalls his grandmother's funeral where, like Camus's Mersault, he is strangely unable to mourn. He has a romantic vision of Monica Alpert, a former girl friend, sitting with him beneath "the oldest tree in the Western Hemisphere," but he is unable to touch her. And through all the windows of all the colleges at which he has studied, Norman looks out to recognize only a "numb cosiness" in himself. The most vivid of these feverish recollections returns finally to the figure of the grandmother:

And, most profoundly, he is being soaked in the words of his grandmother, marinated in the membranous belief she lives by. They sit, just the two of them, on the thousand and one Connecticut nights, listening to the radio and talking during the commercials while winter wind or summer mistral tumbles husband, wild son, arrogant older grandson. And he is all she has, so she preserves him in a shell of *moderation*, warns him against pain, and tells him how he can crawl beneath it and dwell in warmth and safety . . . (p. 81).

Moonbloom awakes from this final vision feeling "weak as a newborn," to find that "something had been torn away from him . . ." (p. 81). When he showers, the water drums on him, "wakening all his nerves," and "even walking was new to him." He leaves his apartment "swaddled" like an infant, to enter "into a strange city."

In the course of the novel Moonbloom makes three rounds of the tenants before dedicating himself to the holy war of rehabilitation. The first of these is followed by the rent-collector's feverish retreat; during the second he has become more attuned to the tenants' cries for help, though he still struggles against the role of confessor they want to have him

assume. When the Chinese sexual athlete Jerry Wung begins to
describe another of his conquests, Norman shouts, "Why are you
telling me all this? Am I supposed to applaud, or what?" (p. 120)
He walks out of the apartment, slamming the door behind him,
but as he does so a Sartrean feeling of "nausea" overwhelms him.
Later, when Sheryl Beeler withholds part of the rent, substitut-
ing for it the promise of sexual adventure, Norman's face is that
of "a long-suffering parent." When the hunchbacked Kram
complains that people sometimes offend him with thoughtless
jokes, Moonbloom replies with "naked honesty": "In a blurred
voice, he said, 'You mean because of your body'" (p. 124). But it
is the aggressive pseudo-intellectual, Wade Johnson, who most
clearly sees the change in Norman: "I detected a tiny glimmer of
passion in you just then. Could it be that the man from the lower
depths is coming out into the light? No more underground, no
more remote control" (pp. 126–27). Later, with bitter but
nonetheless revealing irony, the Jew-hating Ilse Moeller thinks
of Moonbloom as going about his "mission." At the end of this
second round of the apartment houses, Norman returns home
"ashen and crumpled," wondering "whether or not he was at the
bottom of his fearful descent" (p. 147).

Like the electric jolt that flashes through Berman's body,
Norman has, during his second visit to the tenants, received two
blows symbolic of the breaking of his spirit's sleep. As he enters
Wade Johnson's apartment, he is struck in the mouth by a
football, and when he steps through the Hausers' door he is
"assaulted by Carol's screaming rage and then hit by an ash tray
she had aimed at her husband" (p. 146). Nursing these stigmata,
Norman sits down to plan the rehabilitation of the buildings,
taking a comfort familiar in Wallant's writing from the making of
lists, of disciplined codifications which only mark time, delay
temporarily the agony and the joy of his real commitment. Then,
feeling that his identity has been threatened by the events of the
last week, he returns to his hometown as confirmation of the self
he has recalled in his dreams. This central episode of the novel,
recorded in chapter thirteen, is one of Wallant's most contrived
scenes. It is a set piece, a mechanical exercise in the unfolding of
the hero's search for identity, and it dangerously weakens the
novel's imaginative structure. Moonbloom learns, all too predic-
tably, that "you can't go home again," even though he is
temporarily able to recapture the old feeling of emotional

isolationism imparted by his grandmother, and hence to hate "those grasping, importuning tenants, with their filthy illusions, their sickly disguises" (p. 155). But the town he visits—clearly the New Haven in which Wallant, too, was nurtured by female hands—becomes unreal, life-denying: "The occasional people were like shades, the buildings like tombs. His own house was a blur of nothing; downtown, with his favorite luncheonette, was an unlighted slide that revealed contours without life" (p. 155). On the return trip to New York, Norman is accosted by the prophetic candy-butcher, Sugarman, who chastises him, "Ah, Moonbloom, you thought to run away? No dice, little agent; you are hooked, addicted. The withdrawal pains are worse than everything" (p. 156).

V   *A Sense of Mission*

The following week, as he begins his third round of the apartment houses, Moonbloom enters the penultimate stage of his transformation. He accepts a worthless check from Leni Cass, informs Karloff that his filthy apartment will be cleaned and painted and gives the tenants the feeling that he carries "some kind of hope with him. . . ." The accidental death of the Hausers' child fills him with awe. The screams of the mother seem to open up a "ravine" in him; and as the tiny corpse is carried down in the condemned elevator, he stands—in a gesture worthy of Holden Caulfield—trying to shield the obscene drawings on the wall from the stretcher. His old lists of renovations and repairs, his careful columns of estimates for labor and materials, now seem too modest. He makes a new one: "Three hundred dollars for the Hausers for new hearts; six hundred and fifty for Kram's new body; eight hundred and twenty dollars and sixty-six cents for refurbishing Basellecci's dignity; a thousand for a new dignity for Leni Cass; nine hundred for a retread of Ilse's soul; five thousand for a brand-new one for Katz . . ." (pp. 171–72). One recalls that early draft of *The Children at the Gate,* in which Wallant contrasts the mechanical efficiency of urban renewal with the failure of spiritual and emotional renewal. Moonbloom cannot, of course, restore the broken hearts of his tenants, but he can make at least a symbolic gesture at "redeeming" their world, and because his desire springs not from reverence for neatness and efficiency, but from the dawning of love, his crusade is indeed a holy one. In Wallant's original sketch for the novel, this messianic zeal would be prompted by Moonbloom's sexual encounter with one of the tenants, a woman with whom he falls in love and for whose son he has tenderly paternal feelings. In the novel itself Wallant entirely abandons such sentimental motivations. The virginal Norman has his first sexual encounter only after his embrace of the role of redeemer, so that the sexual act itself is a consequence and an affirmation of his joining the human community, rather than a cause. Furthermore, Wallant renders these encounters with the rent-gouging, overblown Shirley Temple in high comic prose. On his first encounter, he has an erection while dancing with Sheryl and arches his body to conceal it from her until he reaches

an extremity of discomfort, and reflexively he snapped erect, plunging like a rivet into Sheryl's kimonoed loins.

"Ohh-hh," he gasped fearfully.

"Ahh-hh," she responded cheerfully.

"I didn't mean . . ."

Sheryl, lovely in the blue-white television light, chucked him under the chin and said, "Let's sit on the couch, hon." She took his hand and led him there, grinning at his stiff, aching walk (pp. 173–74).

When an embarrassed Norman tries to apologize, Sheryl briskly retorts, "Why, honey, all that happened was you got a hard on." Weak with desire, concerned that Sheryl's father may wake up, Norman blissfully agrees to toilet repairs and a rent cut. Presenting him his ultimate reward,

Sheryl raised him higher, her arms extended full length, her face full of savage and delighted mischief. And then she plunged him down, hara-kiri fashion, immolating herself with a great sigh. There was a splat of impact, Norman rolled his eyes back into his head, held on to unimaginable pleasure for a short while, rearing and bucking to the tune of the string section playing *"Bei Mir Bist du Schoen . . ."* (p. 175).

Norman knows now that he has embarked on a "holy war," and he will pursue it with laughter, "for it occurred to him that joy resembled mourning and was, if anything, just as powerful and profound" (p. 176). And for the first time in his life he is able to sing aloud without shame.

Glowing with the spiritual ecstasy that follows his sexual ecstasy, Moonbloom takes "sensual pleasure" in listing the materials he will need to renovate the apartments, happily adjusted to the pain that has settled down in his body and made itself at home." At this moment his resolution is given its first test, when Del Rio, the violent, distraught boxer, comes to announce that he has beaten, perhaps killed, the girl with whom he attempted to release his "tensions." Like Norman, the fastidious athlete was a virgin, but the history to which he confesses is the antipode to Norman's memories of a comforting grandmother. Del Rio sobs out his story: "We lived six in a room, in a filthy, filthy room. My grandmother stank from disease. We saw my father and mother screwing, and when he was only nine and my sister was ten, my brother did it to my sister . . ." (p. 180). Like Lebedov's confession to Angelo, this one calls upon the hero to bear witness; the fact that Moonbloom is closer to redemption than Angelo was is signaled by the mirth that mixes with his feelings of pity and the sense of awe he feels at the new role he plays: "This should have all happened to a bigger man, he thought, a monumental character. It will *kill* me. . . . And the laughter trembled inside him, causing an increase in the pain, which in turn boiled the laughter more rapidly, which increased the pain, and so on" (p. 185). The passage echoes Nathanael West's reflections, in *The Dream Life of Balso Snell,* on the function of laughter:

An intelligent man finds it easy to laugh at himself, but his laughter is not sincere if it is thorough. If I could be Hamlet, or even a clown with a breaking heart 'neath his jester's motley, the role would be tolerable. But I always find it necessary to burlesque the mystery of feeling at its source. I must laugh at myself, and if the laugh is "bitter," I must laugh at the laugh. The ritual of feeling demands burlesque and, whether the burlesque is successful or not, a laugh. . . .[2]

But Wallant's hero laughs not only to protect himself from the crippling pain he would feel if he took too seriously the problems of the Hausers or Del Rio, but because he feels now for all of life such "profound modesty and wonder and shyness."

Tested and found true to his cause, Moonbloom begins what he thinks of as his "jehad," his holy crusade, by cleansing his own dirty office, and the dust flies in comic banishment of the wasteland temperament. Gaylord, Moonbloom's reluctant ally in his crusade, balks at painting the words "Renewers Inc." on the truck they rent to transport tools and supplies, and challenges him with the question, "What the devil you trying to do—make the *world* over?" Norman answers, "Uh huh . . . for me" (p. 191). With the dust rising "chokingly," they scour Karloff's apartment; as Moonbloom labors in kitchens and bathrooms, he becomes "heir to even greater intimacies" from the tenants, for he seems now "as ideal for confidences as a religious image. . . . Maybe he was an ear of God" (pp. 197-98). Fired by his crusade, Norman seems to be growing taller, stronger. The black novelist, Paxton, describes him as a "senile Huck Finn" with a look of agony about him, and Moonbloom retorts that becoming can produce agony, but also joy. Refinishing the floor of the Hausers' vacant apartment, he paints himself into a corner and spends a night-long vigil there, the last trial he will face before the final stage of his transformation. In his final encounter with the tenants, his sense of wonder is preeminent. Eva Baily tries to substitute him for her vanished nephew, asking him to come to dinner and, significantly, eat lamb. Moonbloom's reply is a simple "Ohh-h . . ."(p. 219). Marvin Schoenbrun declares that the mere presence of an air conditioner has taken away his psychosomatic asthma. " 'Ohh,' Norman said" (p. 221). Wade Johnson announces that he and his son are leaving, that they need to be free, and Norman says "Ohh" (p. 222). Leni Cass confesses that it doesn't matter whether her new beau truly loves her or not, so long as she believes he does. " 'Ohh,' Norman said" (p. 222). The Jewish dwarf, after complaining about being rejected by his sister, suddenly asks,

> "You know what kind of house she got, my sister? . . ."
> "No," Norman said dazedly, "no, I don't."
> "Colonial split," Louie said proudly.
> "Ohh," Norman replied (p. 223).

Gripped between Sheryl's legs after an adventurous tour of lovemaking, Norman is suddenly aware that her father is standing beside them.

Like a firing-squad victim, he brought his eyes up to the silver face of Beeler.

"Baby Doll," Beeler said, "you seen my pills, the ones for the arteries?"

"In the medicine chest, Pa," Sheryl said, squeezing Norman in her powerful scissors grip.

"Thanks, Doll Baby," Beeler said tenderly, gazing right into Norman's eyes. "Don't stay up late."

"Good night, Daddy," Sheryl said.

"Driven snow," Beeler said directly to Norman, his weird blue eyes coated with reverence.

"Ohhh-hh," Norman said with great wonder (pp. 223–24).

Ilse Moeller announces that she has converted to Judaism—in short, that she has exchanged her race hatred for a more manageable self-hatred. " 'Ohh,' Norman said" (p. 224). In his last visit to Sugarman, Norman listens to the candy vendor's spiel about a "trinity of survival" that consists of "Courage, Dream, and Love," and once more he replies with a simple "Ohh . . ." (p. 226). Norman's reiterated "Oh's," like the "O's" that are liberated in his name on the window of the real-estate office, are a rapturous expression of that wonder he now feels for the mystery of being. His conversion is ironically paralleled by dramatic changes in the lives of the tenants—Ilse Moeler's conversion to Judaism, Wade Johnson's flight to "freedom" in the American West, the Baldwinesque black writer's departure for Paris, the City of Light.

Despite his brother's threats of dispossession, Norman Moonbloom prepares for the ultimate quixotic gesture, banishing the festering scatology of Bassellecci's toilet wall. The gesture can scarcely help the old Italian, who suffers not from constipation but from incurable cancer. Nonetheless, as an ultimate symbol of the indignities heaped on man, it must be cleansed and renewed. Attempting to persuade his reluctant Sancho Panza to join him in this final mission, Moonbloom argues,

"It's possible that I've become unhinged, deranged. It's very possible. But the way I am now, my former life seems to be the crazy one. That's how far gone I am. It's all those people, Gaylord, all those people. For the first time, people entered me. . . . Some of them are disgusting, some are pathetic. Most of them I don't even like. But they *entered* me, and I don't know how to get them out" (p. 229).

With the assistance of Gaylord and the defrocked Bodien, he almost imagines that he can "pray Bassellecci's wall into transfiguration" (p. 233). Moonbloom's zeal infects not only his two assistants, but the dying Italian as well. The four drink coffee with strega, then strega with coffee, then anisette, Chianti, and vermouth as they attempt to analyze the problem of the bulging toilet wall, and Moonbloom all the while fingers his stigmata, the scar on his forehead. Finally, "ready for levitation," Norman Moonbloom recalls Sugarman's Trinity and attacks the wall with an axe. Drenched in the thick viscosity of filth that spews forth, he howls, "I'M BORN!" (p. 241) To the old Italian he says,

"See, Basellecci, I'm born to you. See, see, smell me, see me. You'll be healed. Everything will be all right!"
"But I'll die," Basellecci squealed in terrible excitement.
"Yes, yes, you'll die," Norman screamed, laughing.
"In terrible pain,"
"In terrible pain."
"Alone?"
"All alone."
Basellecci began to laugh and cry at the same time. "I'm drunk" he wailed. "I'm so drunk that I'm happy" (p. 241).

Indeed, all four men are drunk, and no communion wine was ever more sacred than the one in which they now celebrate man's resources for love and compassion. Moonbloom admits that he is drunk, but knows too that ". . . I'm born and I'm living and I worry and love" (p. 244). When the rosy light of morning begins to tint Bassellecci's "transfigured" wall, Moonbloom returns to the office to await Irwin's arrival, and as he sits there he sees that the last letter of his name has scraped entirely away:

Somehow it freed the word, opened it up so that the o's bubbled out endlessly, carried the crooning sound of the name out to an infinite note of ache and joy. It thrilled him with his own endlessness, and, almost laughing, he followed its course.
Moonbloooo-ooo . . . (p. 245).

VI *Allusion and Literary Analogy*

While allegory still muscles Wallant's vision of man's capacity for redemption, *The Tenants of Moonbloom* is far less dependent than the earlier published novels on biblical-mythical allusion. Instead, the novel rests firmly on the foundation of its brilliant comic conception, and Wallant's own language assumes the burden once somewhat clumsily heaped on an external frame of reference. The allusions and implied parallels that remain are never in danger of inhibiting the felt life of the novel itself; furthermore, the likelihood that they be taken too seriously is considerably diminished by the comic context in which they appear. Norman Moonbloom, former rabbinical student, is the last of Wallant's Christ figures. In his thirty-third year when the events of the novel occur, he experiences rebirth after a feverish "entombment." His sense of messianic mission seizes him at the Christmas season, and his final transfiguration coincides with Easter, which he and his disciples celebrate with communion wine. Moonbloom's mission is predicted by Sugarman, who thus plays the role of John the Baptist or Deutero-Isaiah; the trinity of survival he preaches—"Courage, Love, Illusion"—is an equivalent for the Christian virtues of Faith, Hope, and Charity. But Wallant's Messiah does not, like Christ or Sammy Cahan or Miss Lonelyhearts, end his life in martyrdom, unless we think of the anticipated visit of a fulminating brother as a kind of commercial crucifixion. Nor does Moonbloom redeem the world, or testify to the existence of any beneficent deity; at best, he redeems himself, and in doing so testifies only to the resourcefulness of the human spirit, the transcendent power of man's capacity for love.

Parallel to the Christ motif run allusions to Arthurian legend. On the dusty file cabinet in his office, Moonbloom sketches the single word "Astolat," the name of a legendary Arthurian town, reminding the reader that Wallant's hero searches for a vision of the grail, which he perhaps achieves in burlesque style in the "chalice" of Basellecci's toilet. Moonbloom is accompanied in his search by the black superintendent, Gaylord Knight—a cheerful knight of the roundtable as compared to the sober-faced rent-collector. As a celibate, Moonbloom suggests Galahad; when he surrenders his virginity to the buxom Sheryl Beeler, he recalls Spenser's Red Cross Knight, seduced by the dark-haired Duessa, and he ornaments his lapel with a Red Cross button. Such allusions are made almost parenthetically, and never with the sense that Wallant has attempted to dramatize ancient legend in modern dress, as Malamud does with Arthurian legend in *The*

Natural. Similarly, parallels between Moonbloom and Don Quixote, Gaylord and the sensible, earthy Sancho Panza, serve to highlight the elemental, ageless, and essentially religious nature of Moonbloom's quest, rather than suggesting any precise narrative adaptation.

All such allusions are distilled in Wallant's comic treatment of T. S. Eliot's *The Waste Land,* from which the teacher Wade Johnson quotes to Moonbloom:

> Only
> There is a shadow under this red rock,
> (Come in under the shadow of this red rock)
> And I will show you something different from either
> Your shadow at morning striding behind you
> Or your shadow at evening rising to meet you;
> I will show you fear in a handful of dust.[3]

The passage from Eliot finds frequent comic analogue in the novel; indeed, in Wallant's novels the lonely, dehumanizing spaces in which men spin out their urban destinies are almost always dusty and shadowed, like Nazerman's pawnshop. In *The Tenants of Moonbloom,* however, allusions to Eliot's sere, lifeless landscape are always tinted with comic bravura. Norman writes "Astolat" in the dust on his filing cabinet; the Leopold apartment looks like a picture from "a dusty, old, commonplace album" (p. 49); the boxer Del Rio fastidiously scours away every insinuation of dirt; when Marvin Schoenbrun complains that dust causes his asthma, Moonbloom thinks, "I can no longer stand anything too immaculate. . . . Dust is my destiny" (p. 17). Early in the novel Norman helps Gaylord carry ash cans from the cellar to the street, and the dust unites them: "They went up and down the cellar steps a dozen times with the heavy cans, grunting together, coughing occasionally from the stirred-up dust of the ashes" (p. 28). Moonbloom's tenants are, like the pawnbroker's anguished clients, the crowd of whom Eliot remarks, "I had not thought death had undone so many," and Moonbloom himself is Eliot's wandering knight, his Fisher King, who spends a terrified night in the empty shell of the Chapel Perilous when he shellacs himself into a corner of the Hausers' apartment. Sugarman's trinity of courage, love, and illusion has, as well, its parallel in the Sanskrit words "Datta. Dayadhvam. Damyata." with which Eliot brings the voice of thunder to a close: Give. Sympathize. Control.

The allusions to Eliot's masterwork are no more systematic than those to Arthurian and biblical legend, but they help establish the texture of that landscape in which Wallant's characters exist—its impotence, emptiness, and aridity. In Chapter 7, the only chapter in which Moonbloom himself does not appear, Wallant may have been working a conscious variation on the theme of noncommunication which Eliot explores in the second part of *The Waste Land,* "A Game of Chess." There, a Cockney woman complains the pills she took for an abortion have made her look antique; in Wallant's novel, Eva and Minna Baily listen with horror to Lester's confession that his girl friend is pregnant, and suggest finally that ". . . there are medicines . . ." (p. 85). Tenants meet on the streets or in the hallways of the apartment building, and either ignore each other or communicate only about themselves, never truly registering what the other says. Again and again, the tenants are described as having closed, painted, masked faces; Stan Katz, the jazz trumpeter, has a "tromp l'oeil smile" (p. 20). Sarah Lublin, agonizing over the probable arrival of her husband's overbearing Jewish refugee uncle, meets Jane Sprague before the mailboxes. Jane can only turn her eyes inward in bewilderment at the child she carries, doubtful of her own identity. "I wonder if they really mean me when they write my name on the envelopes. . . . What are your children's names? I forget" (p. 98). The distracted Sarah Lublin answers, irrelevantly, "The apartment is small. . . . It would be peculiar for the children" (p. 95). Later in the day, Bassellecci sees Aaron Lublin in his cubicle at the tax office, and Aaron glances at him "without facial reaction of any kind" (p. 97). And in a final comic gesture to Eliot's theme of sexual impotence as symbol of the failure of spiritual regeneration, Sugarman meditates on a recent failure:

Last night, for the first time in his life, he had been unable to perform with his lady of the evening, and he was near the bottom of his well of inexplicable mourning. Not that the woman had mattered, not that Sugarman had ever planned on perpetuating himself or had ever been concerned with manifestations of his manhood, because he saw himself as a neuterized figure, an implement of this, his humble ritual. . . . Yet somehow that small genital failure, perhaps only a result of weariness and lack of enthusiasm for his partner, had somehow managed to tighten a lid of futility on him . . . (p. 101).

Eliot's poem concludes with only the ambiguous promise of
life-nourishing rain. In Wallant's novels regeneration comes with
fabulous bounty. Furthermore, as the novels progress, Wallant's
heroes become younger, and the tone of the works becomes
increasingly ebullient. Despite his ample literary cousinage—
Christ, Galahad, King Arthur himself, Don Quixote, Leopold
Bloom, Huck Finn, Saul Bellow's Henderson, and Bernard
Malamud's "fixer," Yakov Bok—Norman Moonbloom remains an
impressively original comic creation. His very name suggests his
comic dimension, the improbability of his exalted spiritual
candidacy; it links him to moon-flower, moonshine, moon-struck,
moon-eyed, moon-faced, moony, moonish, to Shakespeare's
"moon-calf" and Jonson's "moonling" or dreamy fool. His heart
heavy with unspent love, like Joyce's Jewish Everyman, Leopold
Bloom, he too wanders the Inferno of the modern city in search
of salvation. Along the way he finds three teachers who attempt
to instruct him—Bassellecci and Wade Johnson, who are literally
teachers, and the candy-butcher Sugarman. Bassellecci is too
turned inward on the disease that consumes him to show
Moonbloom more than the shadow of grace, and the rent-
collector rightly rejects Johnson, with his intellectual prattling
about "that Limey Eliot," as a bad teacher. (In fact, Johnson's
reference to Dylan Thomas's great elegy "Do not go gentle into
that good night . . ." is far closer to Wallant's intention, to the
message Moonbloom is able to give Bassellecci in the conclusion
of the novel). It is Sugarman, Moonbloom's comic *Doppelgänger*,
who recognizes his true vocation, instructs him in its mysteries
and preaches of the essential trinity which Norman will embrace.
Part of the strength with which Moonbloom pursues his destiny
comes from the memory of his own vagabond father, a man who
had rejected the materialist goals that his son Irwin would
eventually champion, and whose rare appearances always
"squeezed a sweet, tart juice through his heart" (p. 31).
Norman's recollection of the joyous night his father appeared to
dance in the snow with his sons is recalled again when he moves
through "swarming flakes" of snow to Bassellecci's apartment.

   With *The Tenants of Moonbloom* Wallant had finally learned,
he said to his wife, Joyce, to be comic without sacrificing
seriousness of purpose. The muted metaphors of change, the
tenuous assertions of father-son recognitions which characterize
the earlier novels, the allusive buttressing of religious themes,

flower in *The Tenants of Moonbloom* into an active comic rage against what Dylan Thomas termed "the dying of the light." It is Wallant's most eloquent revolt against that absurdity which threatens to engulf all his characters. So vividly does he create the anguished existences of the tenants that the reader seems to live in their world, to become a tenant of Moonbloom. No longer the cautious optimist, Wallant had become the comic celebrant of man's capacity to live an energetic, courageous, and spiritually dedicated existence.

CHAPTER 8

"Tannenbaum's Journey"

I *Parents and Children*

HAVING completed two new novels within a single year, Edward Lewis Wallant toyed at least briefly with the idea of returning to the short-story form, and in the last months of his life sketched out some of the ideas he might treat. His rough, uncorrected list reads as follows:

1. Man arguing with father about Eichmann (confusion between good guys and bad)
2. Photographer (Ed Dell) ugly (twisted short arm deaf glasses) yet always surrounded by beauty—"My hero"—Quasimodo—first wife cuckolded him—a natural, nasty buffoon, deeply tormented.
3. Man in SS world who affects his American friend until the American sees the *joy* in the man's reminiscences.
4. "Mystery Writers of America" poor wrecks who write "Sex" books for flea-bag publisher.
5. The "itching" salesman.
6. The Last Effects—brothers going over deceased parents things
7. Man having heart attack while daughter makes love in next room
8. Former carpenter—an American—alcoholic derelict—blamed for sexual assault—beaten to death & then vindicated.
9. Gimple—What Is a Man? Told by son.

The grotesque clearly continued to interest the author, as it had Nathanael West, as a symbol of man's spiritual condition, and so too did the relationship between parents and children. Interestingly, the figure of Gimple once more appears as the possible subject for a further work. None of the short stories was to be written, but Wallant returned to the theme of society's

140

wasted, derelict outcasts in a play he began to write, and Gimple metamorphosed into the lusty figure of Wolfe Tannenbaum. The father-son theme which had engaged Wallant from the beginning of his career as a writer reappears in curious mirror images in the incomplete play and the novel: in *The Way to Spain* a young man seeks his lost father before departing for Europe, and in *Tannenbaum's Journey* an aging father voyages to Europe in search of his lost son.

II   *The Way to Spain*

Wallant lived to complete two of the three projected acts of *The Way to Spain*, a work he originally entitled *Father and Child* or *Going to Spain*. With a backward nod to *The Children at the Gate*, the play is set in the recreation room of "a very small, old and obsolescent veteran's hospital somewhere in New England, half-forgotten officially, run by a skeleton staff and peopled by only a small group of patients."

In December, 1936, a young piano player named Buddy Lewis appears at the home to provide Christmas entertainment for the invalids housed there. He seems, somehow, too talented to take such an engagement, and in his brash, vulgar dialogue he hints that he has for years known of the existence of this obscure hospital and that he has an ulterior motive for coming here. Gradually we learn that the boy's father had deserted his family to join the army in 1917, that he was badly wounded in Europe and sent to this veteran's hospital, registered under the unknown pseudonym he took when he left his family. Buddy intends to fight in the Spanish Civil War, to test and prove his vision of self in much the way that Hemingway's Robert Jordan, still grieving for a suicidal father, proved his. But at this critical moment in his life, Buddy must learn something about the fate of his own soldier father. The theme of the play is articulated in a single brief exchange between the young man and one of the veterans:

Buddy Lewis:	There's a lot of things a guy wants to find out from his old man.
Willy Wilson:	I suppose.
Buddy Lewis:	Things that might tell you something about *yourself,* you know?

Young, talented, irreverent, Buddy Lewis is an effective catalyst for the twelve patients who appear in the play. His entry into the tedious, well-regulated life of the hospital provokes confidences and confessions not only from them, however, but also from the hospital's staff, and again and again what is revealed is the warping of spirit, the terror of loneliness, the failure of real communication. In Wallant's outline for the third act of the play, Lewis finally identifies his father—perhaps in one of the hospital orderlies. He is revealed, however, only to his son, for the brief dialogue between the two was to take place by the dim light of the Christmas tree. Father and son appear only as ghostly, shadowed shapes on the stage.

Wallant's handling of dialogue in *The Tenants of Moonbloom* had demonstrated an uncanny ear for accent and idiom. With dazzling ventriloquism he projected the voices of Italians, Russians, blacks and Jews, with well modulated differentiations for the characters' ages, educations, and social backgrounds. That considerable skill, combined with his growing interest in drama, might well encourage the reader to expect more originality and polish in his construction of *The Way to Spain*. The play's dramatic situation is woodenly contrived, however, and only through the most clumsy manipulations does Wallant succeed in clustering the requisite characters for a given scene in the hospital recreation room. As dramatic settings with a similar function, Nazerman's pawnshop and the Sacred Heart Hospital are managed with far greater theatrical flair. More surprisingly, the play's dialogue is flat and cumbersome, with scarcely a single distinctive inflection that would serve to establish character. One could account for this consistently mediocre performance if it were the simple result of Wallant's failing health. Indeed, the posthumous publication of *The Children at the Gate* and *The Tenants of Moonbloom* led many commentators to presume that all the late work was written under sentence of death. But in fact, Wallant was in full possession of both his health and his creative faculties until nearly the end of his life, as the brilliant manuscript fragment of *Tannenbaum's Journey* richly attests. Wallant's first attempt at playwriting is, to be sure, no less distinguished than his early attempts at writing short stories and novels; had he lived, it might merely have become a setting-up exercise for the drama of Sammy and Angelo he wanted to write, and their story is ripe with theatrical suggestion. The lackluster

qualities of *The Way to Spain* may stem in part from the fact that
Wallant was also engaged in the last novelistic metamorphosis of
Gimple, that ubiquitous celebrant of life who had so long
obsessed him; the genius denied by *The Way to Spain* is
brilliantly reasserted in the novel.

III   *Gimple Metamorphosed*

Two fragments of *Tannenbaum's Journey* survive. The shorter
of them may originally have been intended as a short story,
perhaps the one that Wallant listed among his story ideas as
"Gimple—What Is a Man? Told by son." Here the narration in
fact alternates between a young man, Irving Tannenbaum, and
his father, Wolfe, who lives seventy miles away from his son.
Irving has been raised by his grandfather, his mother, and his
aunt, and nurses continuous resentment for the father who
abandoned them. As the story begins, Irving has accidentally cut
his wrist and his father has for the first time failed to get an
erection with one of his rented girl friends; both receive, in these
simultaneous occurrences, disturbing intimations of mortality.
Later, Wolfe telephones his son, who responds sourly to his
father's expression of interest. Wolfe replies,

"Ah, come on Irving. No, no, I want to *talk* to you—it's important,"
the deep voice said, entering the crack like a wedge.
"Don't speak so loudly, you hurt my ear," Irving said, his voice quite
under control; he hung onto his voice because the rest of him dangled
uncertainly.

Despite his flippant manner and his anger that his mother's
alimony check has not arrived, he reluctantly agrees to meet his
father the following day, and is so nervous that he cannot sleep
that night. He has not yet learned that Wolfe lost the alimony
payment in a poker game.
When Irving's grandfather sees the boy's agitated state, he
tries to talk to him, to heal the breach between father and son:

"He's your father," Louis said, leaning back to observe the effect.
"My father! Oh come on, Louie, stop trying to make me react." Irving
lit a cigarette and dragged deeply on it for warmth. "Sure it unnerves
me a little. I haven't seen him a dozen times since I was six years old and
all of a sudden it's so important for him to talk to me. It puzzles me and

things that puzzle me always make me shaky. A lot of things make me shaky anyhow—I'm a neurotic. But he really is absolutely nothing to me."

"Still and all," Louis said smugly, looking at the windows which were paling in the early winter morning. "A father is a father."

"A father is a father," Irving mimicked. "A father is a father is a father."

Following this exchange, the story bogs down in the grandfather's sententious, sentimental recollections of the exuberant young man who once married his daughter. The conversation which follows, between Irving and his mother, is handled with far greater skill. Wolfe Tannenbaum emerges as a wild and neglectful man, full of energy and an insatiable zeal for life, but one of his rash acts—taking his children out in their pajamas to play in the snow—resulted in a son's dying of pneumonia. On summer nights, too, he had often roused the children to join him in his frolics:

"Or on hot summer nights making us go out in the street in pajamas to look at the stars," Irving's mother complains, "the *stars!* If you could have seen him, heard him—the people in the neighborhood did—all the time raving about light-years and how we were seeing stars that might have been gone for hundreds of years—what did it have to do with us? Yes, raving about them, boasting about them, as though they were *his* stars. . . ."

As he leaves to meet the father who once boasted about the stars, he sees that his acne has returned, as though the prospect of confronting the man has reduced him to adolescence.

This somewhat halting version of *Tannenbaum's Journey* concludes with Irving entering his father's hotel room. Wolfe is in the shower, and while Irving waits for him he looks around at the debris of the old man's energetic life—outsized clothing tossed carelessly about the room, fat leather suitcases, and, spilled from trouser pockets onto the floor, coins, keys, a jackknife, tickets, a package of prophylactics, an immense black comb with broken and missing teeth ("as though it had been used on brillo"), a lollipop and a chestnut. Wolfe at last makes his carefully timed entrance, shouting, "How you *been*, Irving boy?" and whips off his towel "as though to club Irving with his nakedness." It is impossible to determine whether this twenty-

two-page typewritten fragment precedes or follows the more
extensive holograph version of *Tannenbaum's Journey,* though
the latter is composed with such sweeping confidence, and its
variations from the typescript are so significant, that it seems
reasonable to assume that the 150 handwritten pages represent
the author's final thinking about Wolfe and Irving Tannenbaum,
and hence the last work he was to produce in his lifetime.

In the notebook version of the novel, Irving Tannenbaum is
twenty-three years old, a withdrawn young man who has always
lead "a cocoon life," and who opens the novel by absently cutting
a star of David into his wrist at the same moment his father lies in
bed, talking to the woman with whom he has just failed to have
an orgasm. The novel then moves rapidly to the hotel scene in
which Wolfe tauntingly exposes his manhood before his son. The
boy is aggressively cynical, and his father, "impatiently patient,"
vaguely apologetic about his former neglect, but eager to involve
his son in a new business venture. Wolfe hopes to open up the
sporting-goods market in Europe with an "all-sports-in-one"
package designed to relieve the "boredom" of Europeans, and
he needs the educated Irving as vade mecum, translator, and
assistant. When Irving later explains the plan to his grandfather
and mother, their reactions define not only themselves but the
character of the exuberant, careless Wolfe Tannenbaum. The
grandfather's response to Irving's interest in the quixotic scheme
is far less sentimental than in the typescript version. He argues,

"So he's bored with us and himself—let him leave us *and* himself
behind. So he despises his father—let him get it out of his system. You
hate a person like a symbol, a scapegoat. Get up close, live with it for a
while and it gets to be nothing. Maybe Wolfe will just become a stupid
boring man for you—then the *idea* of him won't bother you so much."

Irving plaintively replies, in the name of all of Wallant's
abandoned and fatherless sons, "I don't hate him. . . . You can't
hate nothing."

An anxious Irving departs for Europe in April, and the air is
heavy with spring: "The sun shone on the wet, recently thawed
ground, the trees moved lightly, testingly, with the minute added
weight of buds and the first of the returning birds. The road was
damp and shushed the tires constantly as though enjoining the
respectful quiet due to the hour. A smell of earth came in

through the opened crack of window beside the driver. . . ." To readers familiar with Wallant's fiction, that smell of earth loudly proclaims the eminence of Irving's rebirth, his emergence from the suffocating cocoon of his life, but this time Wallant's treatment of the theme suggests new complexities, for Wolfe confesses to his ex-wife, Goldie, that the ulterior motive of his journey is to look for Leo, his oldest son, who ran away from home years before in protest of "his father's excesses." The noise, confusion, and conflicting emotions that fill the crammed stateroom as the ship prepares to depart seem to draw father and son together, to make them confederates, though Irving still feels strangely fearful of his father's titanic "force."

Made yet more uneasy by the vastness of the sea, the boy is unable to sleep until "finally, he was able to make the small creaks and distant roarings come from the *Santa Maria . . .* and he slept, one with Columbus." The theme of exploration is reiterated again when Wolfe points out that, with their line of merchandising, the two will become "pioneers." Each morning Irving sits on deck reading Dostoevsky's *A Raw Youth,* and each afternoon—a raw youth indeed—he is instructed by an ebullient father in the mysteries of skin-diving, golf, baseball, football, and boxing, the kind of instruction most boys receive in adolescence. It all "seemed some sort of a course in a language Irving could not really fathom. . . ." After this intensive indoctrination in the language of fathers and sons, Wolfe and Irving land at Southampton. The literary youth, thrilled by the thought of this first contact with the Old World, steps off the gangplank onto the cement dock. "Irving said, 'English soil,' and thereupon slipped on some dog feces, fell on one knee into it and broke one of his three pairs of glasses."

Following this scatological debarkation, Wallant's comic voice finds its most robust and inventive range. Wolfe Tannenbaum's hyper sales pitches to stunned conservative English sporting-goods dealers are comic dialogue at its best. Humor never submerges the novel's serious themes, but it creates that necessary perspective the work comes near losing in the opening pages. Wolfe's quest for his lost son remains his central concern; it is even reiterated when Irving slips away for an evening on his own in London and in a pub meets a sailor who has been searching for his brother for seven years. Wolfe, meanwhile, has done his research before leaving America and takes Irving to meet Magid, a Jewish bohemian who once knew Leo. There they learn that Leo has probably gone to Italy, and Irving and Wolfe set off on his trail. When they play poker together on the train, Irving proves himself the better player. Thrilled by this success, he has trouble falling asleep. When he complains, his father answers,

> "I can't sleep either . . . I could use a piece of ass."
> "Don't be disgusting," Irving said.
> "Listen, sonny, I go back a long way—to the beginning of the world. There's nothing disgusting except being dead."

It is a raw tutelage for a raw youth, but gradually Irving will come to respect the spirit if not the letter of Wolfe Tannenbaum's *carpe diem* philosophy.

In Italy a sweating, panicky Irving clumsily translates his father's high-pitched spiel, but realizes he can't sell as his father does. Depressed by this obvious failure in their collaboration, the two visit the Duomo, where Irving begins to explain the work of Michelangelo, and in their mutual fascination with the statue of David, disappointment yields to a contagious enthusiasm. " 'Got a great build,' Wolfe observed, the cases forgotten encumbrances now. 'Built like me when I was younger—no, little longer in the muscles, slenderer—more like Leo. It's beautiful. It looks like he could stand a million years without getting tired.' " Later, Wolfe and Irving get drunk together and leave for Venice, where they have scarcely more success than in Florence, "but they ate and drank well and Irving's acne disappeared leaving him worried about what would replace it." Wolfe is arrested after a midnight swim in a canal, and when he is released he learns from an expatriate American he has met in a bar that Leo has gone to Naples.

The manuscript of *Tannenbaum's Journey* breaks off at this point, and there is no chapter outline to suggest how Wallant's picaresque plot would have evolved. Thematically, however, the novel's rhythms are clearly established. The wolfish Wolfe searches for an heroically ideal son, long-muscled like Michelangelo's David, an athlete and adventurer, and he is accompanied in his quest for the lost lion, Leo, by his sheepish, acned, myopic son Irving. Con-man and randy Don Quixote, Wolfe drags a reluctant Sancho Panza in his furious wake. Yet it is Irving, with the heart of a poet, who is the true heir to Wolfe's vision of life. Once more, no doubt, Wallant would have given us one of his ebullient affirmations, echoing with the laughter that characterizes all his later work. But this time, rather than the reunion of surrogate father and orphaned son, one would have had the thicker reality of the uniting of biological father and son. Such, at least, would seem to be the vision toward which Wallant was moving in his last and most joyous novel.

CHAPTER 9

Symptomatic of His Time

I   *A Humanistic Passion*

THOUGH their estrangement springs from different sources, Wallant's heroes are all alienated people, existing in private limbos which they seek to sustain through hypnotic ritual and emotional narcosis. Their literary cousinage is legion; it includes James's detached observers, Dostoevsky's anguished outsiders, Eliot's Prufrock and Kafka's Joseph K. as well as Saul Bellow's Joseph, Camus's Mersault, and the underground men of Joyce, Sartre, Richard Wright, Ralph Ellison, and Bernard Malamud. The alienated, isolated hero might well be said to have established squatter's rights within the terrain of the modern literary imagination. Stripped of allegiances, he must search for an authentic self without recourse to the conventional props of ideology, religion, or family piety. Indeed, his rescue from the shoals of existential despair rests solely on his ability to find value and meaning within the exacerbated self.

Many such absurd, "dangling" heroes are unable to make the necessary leap into existential faith, to reaffirm any sustaining link of human community. And yet, in the postwar decades, the alienated hero seems to develop a new muscularity, and to conclude his dark night of the soul by proclaiming renewed allegiance to the family of man. Thus Ralph Ellison's Invisible Man announces his intention to leave his snug, well-lit retreat, and Saul Bellow's heroes all conclude their estranged, often chaotic adventures with some ritual gesture that announces the end to alienation. Such works argue that the human spirit is too valuable and too infinitely resourceful to be crushed by nihilism and despair. The pattern was spelled out in Camus's *Myth of*

Sisyphus, a work which has had significant influence on the contemporary literary consciousness, but one which, more importantly, seems to crystallize profoundly the values of postexistential experience. In shouldering the clumsy, insurmountable, and hence absurd burden of his life, Sisyphus heralds the transformation of a new generation of heroes:

I leave Sisyphus at the foot of the mountain! One always finds one's burden again. But Sisyphus teaches the higher fidelity that negates the gods and raises rocks. He too concludes that all is well. The universe henceforth without a master seems to him neither sterile nor futile. Each atom of that stone, each mineral flake of that night-filled mountain, in itself forms a world. The struggle itself toward the heights is enough to fill a man's heart. One must imagine Sisyphus happy.[1]

Such reaffirmations of man's fundamental spiritual capacities begin to appear somewhat sporadically in American writing of the 1950s, and by the end of the 1960s had become a veritable anthem. Their articulation is only the more remarkable when seen against the public agonies of the time—racial strife, political assassinations, technological nightmares, and ecological disasters. To be sure, such darker elements of contemporary experience find expression as well—in the drama of Edward Albee or Imamu Baraka, the anguished private visions of much contemporary poetry, and in the prose of the Black Humorists. Nonetheless, though its landscape is fragmented, often violent, the American novel of the postwar years repeatedly stresses man's capacity for transcendence and regeneration.

The themes of rebirth and renewal, faith in the individual's capacity to make himself anew in his own image, are familiar ingredients of the American literary formula, which from Hawthorne to Salinger and Bellow has presupposed the inevitable recognition of the sustaining ties of brotherhood and community. In the modern American novel, however, the hero's lonely estrangement sometimes grows so acute that hope for any meaningful acknowledgment of what Hawthorne called "the golden chain of humanity" seems perilously thin. Hence the early heroes of Hemingway, the tormented seekers of Nathanael West, the compulsive voyagers of Jack Kerouac rehearse litanies of despair. It is in part that deeply ingrained American optimism, the last shine on the tarnished American Dream, which ultimately saves the American novel from such nihilism. The so-called "new consciousness" of the 1960s no doubt plays its role as well. Malamud's S. Levin, Mailer's Stephen Rojack, and Bellow's Eugene Henderson all bear witness to man's ability to spin out of his own spirit, and in the very jaws of death and decay, a meaningful and authentic existence.

The novels of Edward Lewis Wallant can thus be read as symptomatic of his time—in particular, as representative of the humanistic passion which informs so much Jewish-American writing. His heroes are warped away from any sense of community, becoming defensively jealous of the very isolation which gives them definition. Furthermore, the heroes of Wallant's first two published novels take almost masochistic delight in their burdens of pain, gnawing at their private griefs as a dog gnaws at a wounded paw. But all of these men receive symbolic blows that break the spirit's sleep; shocked into consciousness, torn from their cultivated emotional lethargy, they will consciously choose to declare allegiance to the human fraternity.

II *A Minor Writer with Major Talent*

Throughout this study, parallels have been suggested between the writings of Edward Lewis Wallant and of Nathanael West. Fate suggests yet more: both were Jews, each published four novels, both died as they seemed to be reaching the peak of their creative energies—West at thirty-seven and Wallant at thirty-six. They were intrigued by the nightmare world of the modern city, by the increasingly synthetic nature of contemporary experience, and by the cripples and eccentrics who fight for existence in this ever-thinning air, armored with flimsy disguises and weaponed only with their brittle dreams. The two were also quintessentially comic writers, though West's laughter was bitter and apocalyptic, while Wallant's was increasingly a versatile instrument of joy. The ambiguous confrontations of good and evil, the inevitability of suffering, the role of dreams and the concept of the "sick soul" were concerns they shared, and ones strongly reinforced, philosophically refined, by their reading of Dostoevsky. "We plagiarize constantly, unconsciously," Wallant once wrote, "not merely from all the books which were the illumination, but from the objects that were lighted by them, from existence itself. I did not *read The Death of Ivan Ilyitch*,

The Brothers Karamazov, My Mortal Enemy; I *lived* them."[2]
Nathanael West once argued that if mankind is to survive, the
next two hundred years must belong to Dostoevsky's Chris-
tianity. If by this remark he wished to draw attention to the
Russian's repeated injunction that the individual assume, in love
and pity, the burden of humanity through recognition of a shared
community of men, that he thus reaffirm the substantial identity
of all mankind, it could be argued that Wallant achieved such a
goal in his own fiction more successfully than the "loving
pessimist," Nathanael West. A hastily written note found among
Wallant's manuscripts suggests intimate parallels with
Dostoevsky's love ethic:

What is horrible about not having loved is that one lives in a de-
populated world in which one exists without relevance—that is to say,
all things exist for such a person, only in terms of a single reflection—
that of himself. His relationships with others, if they are not capable of
some selflessness, have no purpose beyond illuminating the single
image. He can be shamed by an unflattering connection to himself and
so his hungers cannot be satisfied for their objects are forever
shifting. . . .

One recalls Dostoevsky's resonant lines from *The Brothers
karamazov,* " 'Fathers and teachers,' I ponder, 'What is hell?'I
maintain that it is the suffering of being unable to love."
    In Wallant's world the failure of love, the arrest of emotional
growth often associated with the early loss of the father, creates
that anomie with which his disappointed heroes try to insulate
themselves from the pain of further bereavement. Emotional
zombies, they sleepwalk through the world until a sudden
blow—not from the hand of God but from the clenched fist of
life—jolts them into wakefulness. The search for self-realization
that follows will teach the sacredness, the awesomeness, of even
the most base experience, and the necessity for a ritual embrace
of the community of man, even when the community seems
atomistic and doomed. With significant minor variations, Wallant's work persistently, even obsessively, follows this mythic
comic pattern. In a great writer we admire such uniformity of
theme and statement as "consistent"; in a lesser one we are apt to
deplore it as "repetitiousness." Inevitably, one cannot entirely
ignore the repetition of novelistic gesture in Wallant's work, and
it marks him as a "minor" writer. Yet his extraordinary growth as

a technician, the rapid flowering within so brief a span of time of his distinctive comic voice, is eloquent testimony to the largeness of his talent. The miraculous transformations which occur in his novels have their parallel in his own transformation from an advertising executive who wrote short stories as a hobby to a dedicated and accomplished novelist.

Wallant's early death affiliates him with the tragic fraternity of American writers who did not live to fulfill the promise of their early works—not only with Nathanael West, but with Stephen Crane, Hart Crane, Isaac Rosenfeld, Theodore Roethke, Randall Jarrell, Sylvia Plath, and Richard Fariña. But Wallant had, at least, the fulfillment of modest but enthusiastic critical recognition of his new vocation, though only two of his novels appeared in print in his own lifetime. Nathanael West's writings were, by contrast, received with almost complete indifference. *The Human Season* was enthusiastically reviewed by *Time* magazine, won the author a fellowship to the Breadloaf Writers Conference, and received both the Jewish Book Council Fiction Award and the Harry and Ethel Daroff Memorial Award for the best novel of the year on a Jewish theme (the Book Council Award would be renamed the Wallant Award after the author's death). *The Pawnbroker*, widely reviewed, was nominated for the National Book Award in 1962 and was immediately optioned for the movies. A Guggenheim Fellowship permitted Wallant to spend five months in Europe, and at the beginning of his journey he stopped in London to discuss the character of his Jewish pawnbroker with Rod Steiger, who would so brilliantly interpret the role in Sidney Lumet's film. Eventually, filmmakers would buy options on Wallant's other three novels as well. Nathanael West, on the other hand, saw his hauntingly surreal *Miss Lonelyhearts* made into a conventional cops-and-robbers film (later cinematic treatments of *Miss Lonelyhearts* and *The Day of the Locust* also failed to achieve real distinction).

While he did not live to see the enthusiastic press his last novels received, Wallant had already enjoyed substantial approbation from critics and reviewers and from such literary acquaintances as Don Wolfe, Charles Glicksberg, John Williams, Richard Yates, Ann McGovern, John Ciardi, and Diana Trilling. To be sure, hardback sales of the novels were modest. *The Human Season* had but a single printing of 4,000 copies; *The Pawnbroker* sold 5,000 copies; the attention accorded the posthumous novels by Wallant's early death accounts for somewhat larger sales—three printings and a total of 8,500 copies of *The Tenants of Moonbloom,* two printings and 7,000 copies of *The Children at the Gate.* The figures are modest, but hardly embarassing. In contrast, Nathanael West's first novel, *The Dream Life of Balso Snell,* was published in an edition of 500 copies; *Miss Lonelyhearts,* published shortly before Liveright declared bankruptcy, was almost immediately remaindered; and West's most successful book, *The Day of the Locust,* sold only 1,486 copies. Embittered by such an indifferent response, West took a job as a Hollywood screenwriter; later, he was unsuccessful in his application for a Guggenheim Fellowship that would have freed him to work intensively on his fiction, even though his candidacy was enthusiastically championed by F. Scott Fitzgerald. Wallant, on the other hand, seemed to be moving rapidly toward the ardent goal of giving his greater energies to a writing career. When he returned from his visit to Europe in the fall of 1962, he believed part-time work in advertising would now be sufficient to supplement his income as a writer—and this only two years after the publication of his first novel.

Following the release of *The Pawnbroker* Wallant had complained that his full and generally routine position at McCann, Erikson, where he worked on accounts for Westinghouse and Bulova, slaked the energies he should have given to his writing. But it would be wrong to cast him in the romantic mold of the sensitive artist who reluctantly sells his soul to the marketplace in order to survive. For most of his life he saw little conflict between his artistic interests and the more routine demands of his public career; he was a responsible, hard-working art director, but his ebullient energy seemed to leave him ample time to study at the New School, to paint, write, and read prodigiously. Only when a belated but zealous sense of literary vocation touched him did he question the bread-and-butter arrangements of his life, and even then, characteristically, he spent less time deploring his situation than making plans to alter it. In the last days before his departure for Europe he heaped together most of his paintings and drawings, as well as various manuscripts and letters, in the backyard of his house in Norwalk and set them alight in a symbolic gesture that would have become one of his own fictional characters. To his wife, Joyce, who protested the fiery destruction, he said simply, "I'll write more for you. I'll paint you other pictures." He had, like his own fictional heroes, acknowledged and embraced his vocation.

III *The One Who Listened*

One searches almost in vain through Wallant's modest biography for the experiences that shaped his penetrating vision of human suffering and loss and ends by concluding that it was his particular genius to draw the largest, most persuasive lessons from the most quotidian sources. He possessed in abundance that vision which for him was the prerequisite of all art:

We speak of art and we speak of illumination; in order to illuminate for others, one must obviously first be able to see for himself. *Seeing* is my key word, seeing with the heart, with the brain, with the eye. I suggest that most people are nearsighted, myopic in their inability to perceive the details of human experience. It is quite understandable; most of us are too busy with survival, with the multitude of things we must do to support ourselves, to live in a community, to have a family. Normally we see others only as they relate to our own immediate needs, and for that, normal vision is often sufficient. Yet there are times when we have a need we cannot recognize, a sudden hunger to know what lies in the hearts of others. It is then that we turn to the artist, because only he can reveal even the little corners of the things beyond bread alone.[3]

Wallant's hometown of New Haven, Connecticut, with its lush green and historic churches, its old, established Jewish community, its revered university, often enters his fictional world — as the setting for *The Human Season* and *The Children at the Gate, for Gimple the Beast,* numerous short stories, and all the early unpublished novels. It is also the hometown to which Norman Moonbloom returns during his crisis of identity. Wallant's contact with Yale University came only through his sales of popcorn and hotdogs at Eli football games, yet it was part of his image of the Connecticut town as a place of stability and tradition; appropriately, his manuscripts were deposited at Yale's Beinecke Rare Book Library after his death. Clearly, the loss of his father was the central trauma of Wallant's childhood and provided him with one of his most recurrent literary themes. Poisoned by mustard gas during the First World War, Wallant's father later developed tuberculosis. Before being transferred to Asheville, North Carolina, he achieved rare visits with his family

156

EDWARD LEWIS WALLANT

only by plunging his thermometer into a glass of ice-water to persuade the doctors that his condition was improving. Edward Lewis Wallant was only six years old when his father died, so that the portrait of the tubercular father in the early manuscript, *Tarzan's Cottage*, would have deeper roots in imagination than in memory. Wallant was raised by his mother, two maiden aunts, his grandfather, and blind grandmother. From the Russian-born grandfather he heard fascinating tales about the old country ("I was the grandchild who listened"), which became the basis for the intensely felt, evocative recollections of Russia in the writer's first published novel.

For a time after he had resigned his studies at the University of Connecticut, Wallant worked in a New Haven pharmacy and like Angelo DeMarco made deliveries to the nearby Catholic hospital. His father-in-law was a plumber, and Wallant was deeply moved by the old man's grief when his wife died; *The Human Season* is dedicated to her—"to Mae Fromkin, who was a plumber's wife, too." At the Pratt Institute in New York he met a Jewish refugee who had survived the Nazi death camps, and though Wallant himself spoke no Yiddish, his friend little English, he somehow contrived to translate for the lonely survivor. In addition to this source for *The Pawnbroker*, Wallant learned from a relative who owned a pawnshop in Harlem, where Wallant used to sit and talk, watching the parade of customers come and go. The author's first visit to Europe immediately inspired new works. London fascinated him; but Italy was his real goal, and he was repeatedly charmed by the country. Despite his anti-Franco sentiments, he liked Spain even better: "Italy was a comic-opera country," he remarked. "I was never scared there. Spain was a tragic country, and the whole time I was there I was scared." "Hell," he remarked to a friend, "is a rainy bus trip through Spain." And yet he felt strangely at home, quickly making friends with artists and writers in Barcelona and excitedly writing in his notebook at the Alhambra. Wallant lost no time in translating his European experiences into fiction, and the uncompleted *Tannenbaum's Journey* is the final demonstration of his uncannily perceptive eye for detail, of his impressive ability to tap the most modest experience or observation until it resounded with the resonant echoes of the creative imagination. Shortly before his death he remarked to his editor, Dan Wickenden, that he could never envision running out of ideas for his fiction, that "his head was stuffed so full of characters and situations and themes that if he lived to be a hundred there would still be more to write about."[4]

Had Wallant lived to submit more of those characters and situations to the processes of imagination, it would almost certainly have been unnecessary to speak of him as a "minor" novelist, for his compassionate understanding was clearly that of a major artist. At moments it would seem as though Wallant personally assumed the challenge laid down to his generation in William Faulkner's Nobel Prize acceptance speech:

Our tragedy today is a general and universal physical fear so long sustained by now that we can even bear it. There are no longer problems of the spirit. There is only the question: When will I be blown up? Because of this, the young man or woman writing today has forgotten the problems of the human heart in conflict with itself which alone can make good writing because only that is worth writing about, worth the agony and the sweat.

He must learn them again. He must teach himself that the basest of all things is to be afraid; and, teaching himself that, forget it forever, leaving no room in his workshop for anything but the old verities and truths of the heart, the old universal truths lacking which any story is ephemeral and doomed—love and honor and pity and pride and compassion and sacrifice. . . .[5]

Wallant's subjects were precisely man's capacity for compassion, sacrifice, and endurance, and far more assertively than Faulkner's own novels, his suggest that humankind will prevail. Despite their persuasive air of contemporaneity, the novels are curiously old-fashioned in their recurrent, passionate concern with man's capacity for rebirth and regeneration; emotive, increasingly sanguine, they are uniquely "nonintellectual" works for a Jewish novelist. Their emblematically ordinary characters at first seem frail standard-bearers for the proclamations the author would make, as Wallant himself must have sensed when he attempted to bolster them with allegory. But as confidence in his craft rapidly developed, he would permit his characters increasing independence of such overtly literary manipulations, with the result that his later heroes articulate the author's message of compassion and community with increasing joy and authenticity. One laments the unfinished and the unwritten novels, plays, and short stories, but it is far more appropriate to

Wallant's celebrant vision to rejoice in the works he lived to write, in the old verities and truths of the heart he there made manifest.

Notes and References

Chapter Two

1. All quotations from Wallant's unpublished manuscripts are taken from the papers on deposit at the Beinecke Rare Book Library at Yale University.

2. The alternate version of the story shows the narrator returning home, following the revelation of gluttony and love, with a "harsh, iron taste of impoverishment, and his loneliness seems like a bare corridor leading off to an emptiness so terrible it will drive him mad." He calls up a former girlfriend, arranges the apartment for a seduction scene, and feels "a sort of horror" when she arrives looking like "a bright, enameled machine." In the end, he tries unsuccessfully to convince himself that this bachelor existence is preferable to the trap of marriage.

3. In one draft of the novel Wallant gives the family the name "Middleman," and the name suggestively appears in other unpublished works as well. Note, also, Ber*man* and Nazer*man*.

Chapter Three

1. Theodore Dreiser, *Sister Carrie* (New York, 1932), p. 554.

2. Rabbi Solomon Ganzfried, *Code of Jewish Law* (New York, 1961), p. 130.

3. Ibid., p. 129.

4. "The Agony of Choice: Dialectic in the Novels of Edward Lewis Wallant," unpublished doctoral dissertation (The University of Wisconsin, 1972), pp. 38–39.

5. *The Magic Barrel and Other Stories* (London, 1960), p. 28.

6. Archibald MacLeish, "Einstein," *The Collected Poems of Archibald MacLeish* (Boston, 1962), p. 258.

Chapter Four

1. *Anatomy of Criticism* (Princeton, 1957), p. 215.

Chapter Five

1. *Men and Letters: Essays in Characterization and Criticism* (Boston and New York, 1877), pp. 131–32.

2. Bernard Malamud, *The Assistant* (New York, 1958), pp. 99–100.

3. *The Stories of Anton Chekov*, ed. Robert N. Linscott (New York, 1932), p. 6.

4. "The Love Song of J. Alfred Prufrock," *The Complete Poems and Plays of T. S. Eliot* (New York, 1952), p. 7.

5. The prologue to Eliot's "Prufrock," taken from Dante's Inferno (xxvii, 61–66), translates: "If I believed my answer were being made to one who could ever return to the world, this flame would gleam [i.e., this spirit would speak] no more; but since, if what I hear is true, never from this abyss did living man return, I answer thee without fear of infamy".

6. Eliot, *Complete Poems*, p. 39.

7. Most of the actions and the dialogue attributed to the pawnbroker in this outline of the novel are too emotionally demonstrative, too dramatic, to fit the essential concept of the character. In pruning and concentrating the action of the final scenes, Wallant clearly intensified the dramatic impact of the novel. But in the outline for Chapter 19 one sees the germ of Sammy Cahan's impassioned plea for love in *The Children at the Gate*. Typically, an idea or situation abandoned in one novel becomes the source for another.

8. The very language in which Wallant describes the deaths of David and Jesus reinforces the parallels between these two "sons." As David slips to the floor at his feet, Sol *"tried to move a little more than his fingers, felt the soft-damp hair of David's head as it slid slowly downwards."* After the fatal shot is fired in the pawnshop, Sol becomes aware of "a human body, sliding slowly downward. . . . His hand pressed on the clothed, warm figure, tried to keep it from falling. It slid under his hand."

Chapter Six

1. *The Complete Poems and Plays of T. S. Eliot*, p. 65.

2. For the analysis of names in the novel, I am indebted to the very thorough research of William V. Davis, in his doctoral dissertation *Sleep Like the Living: A Study of the Novels of Edward Lewis Wallant* (Ohio University, 1969), pp. 79–81.

3. *One Flew Over the Cuckoo's Nest* (New York, 1962), p. 17.

4. Such problems in the manuscript account for its being published after *The Tenants of Moonbloom*, though actually written first. Harcourt, Brace received so many requests for information about Wallant following his death that Dan Wickenden prepared a biographical sketch, which was distributed in mimeographed form. It explains the problem of the sequence of the last two novels as follows:

As to which of the two posthumously published novels was written first, the situation is a little complicated, though to all intents and purposes it can be said that *The Tenants of Moonbloom* was the last book Ed wrote. *The Children at the Gate* and *Tenants*, both written within the same twelve months, were submitted to us (again) almost simultaneously early in 1962, because Ed wanted to know our opinion of both of them before he left for Europe. As I recall, he had spent six or eight months writing, then rewriting, then rewriting for a second time *The Children at the Gate:* it came hard to him, and meant more to him than any of his other books. *The Tenants of Moonbloom* came rapidly, with the utmost spontaneity, and what Ed submitted to us was what he called a rough first draft, although it was in fact a second draft. (His custom was to write, first, a detailed outline; this he would develop into a skeletal narrative; the fleshed out narrative based on this was what he considered a first draft.) We felt, rightly or wrongly, that *The Tenants of Moonbloom* was ready for publication pretty much as it stood, but that *Children* still needed more polishing. We also felt that it might be better to publish *Moonbloom* first in any case, because it seemed a greater departure from the earlier books than *Children* did.

Ed agreed to this schedule, and took copies of both manuscripts with him to Europe, where he worked on both of them. The changes in *Moonbloom* consisted chiefly in the deletion of two or three characters—other tenants—who were less well drawn than most. The final cuts and changes in *Children* were far more drastic. He returned to the USA at the time of the Cuban crisis (his wife and children had preceded him, to be ready for the opening of school), and delivered the revised version of *Moonbloom* immediately. A copy of *The Children* manuscript with his final revision did not come into our hands until after his death, early in December, 1962; and we decided to abide by the publishing schedule to which he had agreed.

It should be noted, however, that further editorial revisions of *The Children at the Gate* were necessary—a final indication of the problematical nature of the novel. Dan Wickenden observes that Wallant's last version of the novel still contained numerous "excesses (two adverbs for every verb, two adjectives for every noun, a proliferation of similes ranging from inspired to impossible, and a whole very bad Chapter, clumsily and pedestrianly written, about Angelo and his sister and an excursion to the beach, whose chief purpose, I suppose, was to underline a certain incestuous attachment between the siblings . . .)." Letter from Dan Wickenden to David Galloway (March 1, 1976).

Chapter Seven

1. Nathanael West, *Miss Lonelyhearts, The Complete Works of Nathanael West* (New York, 1957), p. 106.
2. *The Dream Life of Balso Snell*, ibid, p. 27.
3. *The Complete Poems and Plays of T. S. Eliot*, p. 38.

Chapter Nine

1. Albert Camus, *The Myth of Sisyphus,* trans. Justin O'Brien (New York, 1959), p. 91.

2. "The Artist's Eyesight" (New York, 1963), unnumbered. These remarks are drawn from an essay Wallant prepared for a Harcourt series designed to be used by teachers. The essay gives us Wallant's sole public commentary on the art of fiction, as well as the only available details about his reading preferences.

3. Ibid.

4. Dan Wickenden, "Edward Lewis Wallant," p. 3.

5. William Faulkner, "Nobel Prize Acceptance Speech," *The Portable Faulkner* (New York, 1967), pp. 723-24.

Selected Bibliography

1. Novels

The Children at the Gate. New York: Harcourt, Brace and World, 1965.
The Human Season. New York: Harcourt, Brace and World, 1960.
The Pawnbroker. New York: Harcourt, Brace and World, 1961.
The Tenants of Moonbloom. New York: Harcourt, Brace and World, 1963.

2. Short Stories

"I Held Back My Hand," *New Voices 2: American Writing Today,* ed. Don M. Wolfe. New York: Hendricks House, 1955.
"The Man Who Made a Nice Appearance," *New Voices 3: American Writing Today,* ed. Charles I. Glicksberg. New York: Hendricks House, 1958.
"When Ben Awakened," *American Scene: New Voices,* ed. Don M. Wolfe. New York: Lyle Stuart, 1963.

3. Essay

"The Artist's Eyesight," *Teacher's Notebook in English.* New York: Harcourt, Brace and World, 1963.

Ayo, Nicholas. "Edward Lewis Wallant, 1926-1962," *Bulletin of Bibliography,* 23 (October-December 1971), 119. The Wallant bibliography lists all primary and secondary materials published before 1971.
———."The Secular Heart: The Achievement of Edward Lewis Wallant." *Critique: Studies in Modern Fiction,* 12 (1970), 86-94. As well as pointing out parallels between Wallant's writings and those of Flannery O'Connor, Dostoevsky, Saul Bellow, and Bernard Malamud, Ayo stresses the entire secular nature of the spiritual quest on which Wallant's heroes embark.
Balliet, Whitney. "Lament," *New Yorker,* 40 (September 19, 1964), 210-11. Written shortly after the publication of *The Children at the Gate,* this review-article offers a sensitive, balanced appraisal of Wallant's achievement.

163

BAUMBACH, JONATHAN. *The Landscape of Nightmare: Studies in the Contemporary Novel.* New York: New York University Press, 1965, pp. 138–51. Entitled "The Illusion of Indifference," Chapter 9 concentrates on *The Pawnbroker,* with particular stress on the "ritual structure" of the work.

BECKER, ERNEST. *Angel in Armor.* New York: George Braziller, 1969, pp. 75–100. Chapter 3, entitled "The Pawnbroker: A Study in Basis Psychology," contrasts Wallant's novel with the filmscript written by Morton Fine and David Friedkin. The latter, according to Becker, is more Christian than Judaic in its conclusion. Becker repeats the common (and erroneous) presumption, inspired by the author's early death, that Wallant "literally squeezed [his] insight out of his own living flesh and consumed himself in the process."

DAVIS, WILLIAM V. "Fathers and Sons in the Fiction of Edward Wallant," *Research Studies* (Washington State University), 4 (1972), 53–55. One of several articles excerpted from Davis's doctoral dissertation, this stresses the centrality of the father-son relationship in Wallant's novels.

———. "Learning to Walk on Water: Edward Lewis Wallant's *The Pawnbroker.*" *Literary Review,* 17 (1973), 149–65.

———. "The Renewal of Dialogical Immediacy in Edward Lewis Wallant," *Renascence,* 24 (1972), 59–69. *The Human Season* is analyzed in detail as providing the nucleus for Wallant's fictional canon.

———. "Sleep Like the Living: A Study of the Novels of Edward Lewis Wallant," *Dissertation Abstracts,* 28:3177A (Ohio University, 1969). Davis's dissertation, though somewhat naive in its critical methods, contains a good deal of useful background information on Wallant's novels.

———. "A Synthesis in the Contemporary Jewish Novel: Edward Lewis Wallant." *Cresset,* 31 (1968), 8–13. A brief biographical sketch and a summary of the themes of the novels are followed by a discussion of the broadly humanistic tradition in which Wallant is situated. Martin Buber and Paul Tillich are stressed as Jewish and Christian "synthesizers" of that tradition.

FEIN, RICHARD J. "Homage to Edward Lewis Wallant," *Midstream,* 15 (May 1969), 70–75. This article stresses Wallant's treatment of the urban American Jew as comic "savior."

GALLOWAY, DAVID D. "Clown and Saint: The Hero in Current American Fiction," *Critique,* 7 (Spring-Summer 1965), 46–65. Wallant's characters are analyzed as part of a contemporary comic tradition which also includes Stanley Elkin, Terry Southern, Joseph Heller, Saul Bellow, and John Hawkes.

GREENBERG, HAZEL. "Cluster Imagery in the Novels of Edward Lewis Wallant," *Dissertation Abstracts,* 33:5176A (Southern Illinois,

1972). This is a precise and searching analysis of the imagistic structuring of Wallant's novels.

GURKO, LEO. "Edward Lewis Wallant as Urban Novelist," *Twentieth Century Literature*, 20 (October 1974), 252-61. Gurko sees Wallant's novels as representative of a heightened concern for the urban experience in America.

HOYT, CHARLES ALVA. "The Sudden Hunger: An Essay on the Novels of Edward Lewis Wallant," *Minor American Novelists*, ed. C. A. Hoyt. Carbondale: Southern Illinois University Press, 1970, pp. 118-37. In discussing Wallant's relegation to the status of a "minor" writer, Hoyt brings together much useful biographical data, as well as offering a straightforward, persuasive analysis of the novels.

KLEIN, MARCUS. "Further Notes on the Dereliction of Culture: Edward Lewis Wallant and Bruce Jay Friedman," *Contemporary Jewish American Literature*, ed. Irving Malin. Bloomington: Indiana University Press, 1973, pp. 229-47. Klein sees Wallant's work as "liturgical and melancholy" and objects that the author does not "test" his own vision sufficiently.

LEWIS, ROBERT W. "The Hung-Up Heroes of Edward Lewis Wallant," *Renascence*, 24 (1972), 70-84. Lewis sees Wallant as a "meliorist determinist" and a representative—together with Hubert Selby, Jr., and John Rechy—of the "new naturalism."

LORCH, THOMAS M. "The Novels of Edward Lewis Wallant," *Chicago Review*, 19 (1967), 78-91. The article is noteworthy as one of the earliest critical appraisals of Wallant's achievements as a novelist.

LYONS, JOSEPH. "*The Pawnbroker:* Flashback in the Novel and Film," *Western Humanities Review*, 20 (Summer 1966), 243-48. Lyons stresses the successful use of cinematic technique in transmitting Wallant's intentions in *The Pawnbroker*.

ROVIT, EARL. "A Miracle of Moral Animation," *Shenandoah*, 16 (Summer 1965), 59-62. Rovit concentrates on Wallant's "perverse fascination for the most unlikely fictional materials" and his recurrent use of "initiation archetypes."

RUDDEL, JOYCE. "The Agony of Choice: Dialectic in the Novels of Edward Lewis Wallant," *Dissertation Abstracts International*, 32:5804A (Wisconsin, 1972). Rudell's dissertation is a sensitive and intellectually rigorous approach to the novels, stressing Wallant's skill as a craftsman and his increasingly complex humanistic vision.

SCHULZ, MAX F. "Wallant and Friedman: The Glory and the Agony of Love," *Critique*, 10 (1968), 31-47. Wallant's novels are seen as *Bildungsromane* and compared to the works of Bruce Jay Friedman in their vision of the human experience of love.

STANFORD, RANEY. "The Novels of Edward Wallant," *Colorado Quarterly*, 17 (1969), 393-405. Stanford urges that Wallant's exceptionally mature work not be neglected because of his early death and supports his plea with a competent, if somewhat pedestrian, analysis of the novels.

Index

167